WALKING FOR BREEZES TOGETHER

JAMES NELSON CAULKINS

Outskirts Press, Inc.
http://www.outskirtspress.com

ISBN: 978-1-9772-0362-5

Cover Illustration by Kirsten Guerrero. All rights reserved - used with permission.

Outskirts Press and the "OP" logo are trademarks belonging to Outskirts Press, Inc.

PRINTED IN THE UNITED STATES OF AMERICA

This book is dedicated to my wife and friend, Lorna,
whose compassionate heart adds quality to my life.

And to all the explorers out there.

Introduction

OVER A CENTURY from now the world of people has changed, but the earth still revolves around the sun year after year, tilts season after season, and rotates on its axis day after day. God has not struck down humanity for its sins, nor has the earth shrugged off humanity as though curing an illness. It's people who have hurt themselves. And many people have learned from humanity's self-destructive drives. Drives toward war, hatred, anger, bigotry, and intolerance. Many people have learned humility. They've learned that air, water, and soil pollution is no more than animals fouling their own nest. Individual nests were clean; humanity's was not. They've learned responsibility. They've learned that population unchecked by reason is no more than animals breeding. Families were healthy; the human race was not. They've learned kindness. They've learned that violence, division, hatred, and crime exist on one side of a perspective and that maturity, compassion, and tolerance are on the other. That side can be found and lived through no more than an awareness and individual application of the commonly known concept of "do unto others."

The living of that simple concept on an individual level has allowed many people to embark on a learning journey that has taken them to some consequential truths. Truths like the heart and mind are not separated. They've learned that the body and soul are not separated here on Earth. They've learned that living with separations between heart and mind, body and soul, reason and feeling, causes

i

a schizophrenic-like division in individuals. They've learned that reason and feeling are two sides of the same coin. That coin is each one of us. The learning did not come quickly or easily. Arrogance caused individuals to miss the basic cause of their own problems.

The divisions that existed in individuals were reflected in countrywide divisions also, as a country is made of its individuals. Divisions between races, religions, left and right, capitalism and compassionate sharing grew from the divisions in individuals. Those countrywide divisions influenced how this Country of Freedom interacted with other countries. This Country, the Country of Freedom, led the world and so led the problems that hurt the world. This Country of Freedom waited too long to pull back its weapons from the world, waited too long to learn that the part of capitalism dependent on selling weapons of war is a failure of diplomacy not a profit. Waited too long to choose to freely reach out to the world with its clean air, clean water, medical, industrial, and computer technologies. This Country waited too long to reach out to others while giving no thought to profit except the gain of international goodwill, waited too long to grow above greed to compassion. This Country of Freedom waited too long to change its chosen dependency on other countries' energy to the freedom of energy independence. In their own ways, other countries did no better. Individuals everywhere lived with divisions between heart and mind, causing divisions between people, which caused divisions between countries. The organized religions did not help with these divisions. They only taught people to focus on obedience to their own dogmatic structure and affiliation to their own beliefs, thus creating religions' own divisions in people. Divisions that persisted until people learned that when God created man in His image it means that God created humans as self-determinate beings. Because when a being is self-determinate, as God by definition is, all other images of one's self are secondary.

Humans have not done well with this gift of self-determination, which results in ultimate freedom. They have not done well with the freedom to create their own destiny and their own individuality. They chose to worship God rather than to love mankind. They chose to believe that what is better will be given to them by something greater than they. Too few chose to create a better world for all humanity by their own individual effort, their own individual intent. People did not realize that the tough questions for them to answer, the questions whose answers contain enough responsibility to create individuality, have been put into organized religions and then glossed over with obedience and worship. They did not realize this until, with individual intent, they learned to bring reason into religion and so build their own individuality. An individuality tempered by the awareness of each person's own humanity. An individuality that unites heart and mind, body and soul, reason and feelings. An individuality that causes belief and faith to shift to a firmer foundation but not to be replaced by information and reason. A belief and faith in one's self and one's own individual connection to God instead of belief and faith in authority figures, their constructs, or institutions. The people in this Country of Freedom, not all, but many, have learned that the freedoms granted to each individual by their own Constitution could best be lived through the development of value systems, codes of ethics, or religions, from an individual perspective with an awareness of humanity. Not all, but many have learned this. And they have let their voices be heard and they teach their children. The voices of obedience, oppression, and authoritarianism are not gone, but the light of freedom and individuality shines on them and is pushing them into the shadows where they belong.

This is today's world for the individuals of tomorrow. The world that the individuals of tomorrow have the privilege of being the guardians for and of determining their future in. Individuals whose intent creates their perspective and whose experiences are appraised by their own chosen value systems. They are individuals whom God has given the ultimate gift of self-determination by creating them in his image. They are individuals for whom the gift of dominion over life on Earth is a debt owed, a responsibility, not an opportunity. They are individuals for whom Jesus of Nazareth is one in a line of wise men which includes Buddha, Confucius, and Mohammad. Wise men who deserve respect and whose teachings should be applied to individual lives through intent. These individuals in tomorrow's world freely choose to intend to unite heart and mind, body and soul, reason and feelings. They are individuals who apply the freedoms written into law in this country's Constitution on an individual level.

Chapter One

HE FEELS PACKED earth under his bare feet. It's easy to walk quietly on an often-used path. Looking from behind a large willow shrub, where he always does, to see what's out in the open, Anoo looks around for several minutes. Some small dimples on the water's surface in closer to shore than the sluggish August current, minnows. Dragonflies, violet-green and barn swallows, out hunting on a hot afternoon, expected. It looks like it did yesterday here at the river's edge. Stepping out from behind the willow he walks out on the gravel bar he always uses for his afternoon swim. Stripping off his sweaty work clothes he wades out into the water. It's tepid in the shallows but cooler as he goes out deeper. He dives out and swims to what current there is, then dives down into water just over his head. At the bottom he grabs hold of his favorite rock. It has handholds and is in the perfect spot. It's in the deepest part of the pool with the most current and the coolest water. It's the perfect rock in the perfect spot because he put it there. He looks around, normal murkiness. Staying under a full minute he lets go and surfaces. Water runs off his face. His lungs fill with fresh air and he goes down again. He's done this too many times to count and it still feels wonderful. As do his muscles as he surfaces and swims around the pool several times. The cooling breeze on his naked body as he walks out of the water, a delight each and every time.

Sitting on the gravel bar he thinks of his day. First some leftovers to eat from the night before, then a walk around the farm with the dogs. There are no problems from the night. Water is given to all the animals. Then the chickens and turkeys are let out to scratch, the horses and cows to pasture. After that he adds to the compost pile with what he mucks out of the animals' stalls. Next, it's time to pick produce. The fall harvest hasn't started yet but there is still plenty to do. What's ripe and ready goes in the house to be cleaned and stored. What's buggy, overripe, or thinned goes to the pigs. His father, Eli, has started the cookstove and then gone out and checked the orchard and is picking crops also. He's already taken an assortment of vegetables in for his wife and Anoo's mother, Tohlee, to prepare for a lunchtime soup. With that simmering on the stove and fresh bread baking in the oven she's now working next to the house amongst her herb, flower, and medicinal plant beds. After the produce is picked the animals reluctantly go back into their stalls. It's always too soon for them; they want to stay out eating all day. Anoo eats lunch and then the extra produce is cleaned and stored. Now he's at the gravel bar on a beautiful afternoon. Another beautiful afternoon, another refreshing swim, delightfully naked in the sun again, by himself.

As he sits he thinks about his life and the farm. It's a good life but it is his parents' farm. He's welcome here but he wants something more. Town is good because of his friends there, but it's town. His great-uncle Mateen's life, solitary in the hills, is good, but it's not a young man's life. Being a scholar in the city would mean leaving behind the natural world he connects his philosophy to. He knows he can spend a lifetime learning here. The river, the farm, the wildlands beyond. Looking larger, looking smaller, asking the right questions, experimenting. There's always more to learn when self-motivated. He knows no answers will come to him today. May as well sit and enjoy this mid-August afternoon. The Perseids meteor shower will be peaking over the next few days. A visit to Mateen's cabin? That sounds good. Higher elevation and so clearer skies to watch the show. It's not an answer to his concerns about his future, but a change. This is a good time for a break. The main fall harvest won't start until September. He can talk over the idea with his parents during dinner, which will be fresh sautéed vegetables and meat stored from last fall's hunt. The food is healthy and good and yet familiar. Yes, time for a visit with Mateen. Tomorrow, work here, then to town and his friends for the night. From there, the full day hike up to the cabin.

Another walk to town for Anoo. It's still hot in the early evening but it's always a nice walk. Rain, snow, cold, hot, it's always a nice walk. A dog barks from a nearby farm, the excited bark of a dog playing. A magpie squawks in the distance; they're very vocal. He sees a nearby flash of blue and black and stops as a Steller's jay lands on a branch next to the road. It's close enough for him to see the white lines on its face pointing at him. Walking on, he sees a doe and fawn cross the road. How many has he seen? Way too many to count and yet the form of the doe as she jumps the fence by the road causes him to stop and watch. So strong, deliberate, and free. Free even though she's chosen the concerns of having people nearby. Freedom from wolves and mountain lions. Freedom enough to bear and raise her young. Her fawn pokes its head through the fence and then wiggles its body through. A few more weeks added to its new life, a few more games of tag with its mother and it will jump the fence for the sheer delight of it. Farther ahead, past the deer, two neighbors come out onto the road from their lane. They're headed to town too. He gives a quick wave letting them know not to wait for him. He'll have plenty of company tonight. It's always nice to walk to town. Every time, the many times.

Anoo enjoys the visit with his friends. They're working the next few days, so he's off on his own to the cabin. After a quick breakfast, he puts on his pack and heads out the door. It's light but the sun isn't quite up yet. He climbs up and over the dam at the far end of town where he sees an acquaintance fishing in the little reservoir. He waves and keeps going. Walking along the shore he enjoys the play of the sunrise colors reflecting off the water and how the colors dance with the ripples of the morning breeze.

At the inlet to the reservoir Anoo starts uphill. After a short walk through tall shrublands he finds the trail that runs along the top of a little ridge. It's rocky and blasted by the summer sun here but the trail will take him a couple miles in to the comfort of walking under aspen trees. As he's walking he thinks about his great-uncle Mateen. He knows Mateen traveled around for years as a young man, mostly to the west of Colorado. Mateen's hometown, and Anoo's now, was Mateen's home base. It's a small town more than a hundred miles northeast of Denver. Mateen had a brother Mikhail, who was Anoo's grandfather. Mikhail was not the wanderer that Mateen was. He spent his life in their hometown, married his childhood sweetheart Rosario, and had a child, Eli, Anoo's father. Unfortunately, some half-dozen years after Eli was born Rosario died in childbirth. Her daughter didn't make it either. After helping Mikhail adjust to his tragically altered life Mateen started traveling again. Mining camps and towns built around ranching were familiar to him. He could always find a little work before moving on.

During one visit home Mateen lets his brother know he wants to see the ocean and doesn't expect to be back for several years. With a farewell to his brother and nephew, off he goes. His trip takes him to San Francisco and the great ocean. Intrigued by something so big and new to him he takes a sailing ship to Hawaii. On the return trip he comes ashore in Los Angeles and then takes a southerly route to Colorado. Back in his little hometown after several years absence he finds that his brother has been hurt some months before, in a farming accident. With Mikhail unable to run his farm and Eli needing help, Mateen settles in to farm life. After enduring his crippling injury for a couple of years Mikhail passes away. A few years later, when Eli is sixteen, Mateen gets the urge to wander some more and takes his nephew with him on some adventures.

After wandering for a few years Eli decides he's more like his father and goes back to his hometown to make his life. He's content for a while being a single man and working on other's farms. Then he meets Tohlee; they fall in love and marry. They decide they want to live on Mikhail's old farm, which has fallen into disrepair. Mateen helps them get the property up and running again and then moves to a cabin up in the hills. He still travels around some but is older and more settled.

About ten years after marrying, Eli and Tohlee have a son they name Anoo. For the first few years after Anoo is born Mateen is often at the farm helping out. As Anoo grows, Mateen's visits change to spring and fall. He helps with spring planting and the fall harvest. After the fall harvest Eli, Tohlee, and Anoo go to the cabin for a fall hunt. When Anoo is fourteen his parents and Mateen decide he should spend some time with Mateen exploring the far reaches of the hills above the cabin. Anoo's walkabout with his great-uncle brings them closer. After the walkabout Anoo visits Mateen when farm work allows. Now, at twenty-one, Anoo finds himself on another trip to the cabin and wondering where he should direct his life.

"Hello, Mateen!" Anoo calls out as he comes in sight of the cabin.

"Hello there, my young friend. You don't have to yell so loud. Even the grouse heard you coming and got out of the way."

"I didn't want you to mistake me for a revenuer looking for your still."

"Well, I'm not distilling but that doesn't mean we can't do some swilling!" Mateen laughs.

They settle into the Adirondack chairs on the back porch with some moonshine and look east from Mateen's cabin down to the willows and beaver ponds at the bottom of the small valley running from south to north below them. Across the valley ponderosa pines and large junipers dominate the west-facing hillside. It's late afternoon and the shade of the porch is cool and welcoming after Anoo's walk. The roughly fifteen miles from town is a nice day's hike for him.

"Did you have a nice walk?"

"It's been a beautiful day for a walk. A little warm after mid-morning but nothing your spring-fed shower won't cure."

"Last night your father said you were coming today. Give me a minute and I'll let him know you've arrived safely."

With that Mateen looks off in the distance. Anoo knows what he's doing. He's visualizing Eli and remembering the feeling of their shared friendship. He's making a connection with Eli through his mind. Anoo wonders what is actually connecting. Is it mind to mind? They are each aware of the other. It's the same time of day for each individual. But distance isn't a factor. How can distance not be a factor? No more time passes than if Eli were here and they were talking aloud. What kind of a connection is this? After a few seconds Mateen laughs and sits up straight.

"Well, there was no reason for a long conversation. Your parents are down by the river at the swimming hole."

"You don't have to explain. I know what they like to do there." Anoo laughs.

"And what about you? Is there a woman in your life?"

"Just the women in town I've known all my life. I don't think they're lifelong for me or something more would have grown between us already."

"What brings you here today, my young friend?"

"Things are a little quiet at the farm these days. Everything is growing without needing much tending. So, I thought a little visit, the coolness of your aspen grove, and a couple nights of the meteor shower would be nice."

"You'll have clear nights and the moon will be down early, so good timing. Where will you watch from?"

"I'm thinking that high spot six or so miles from here that is too rocky for trees. I'll be able to watch the whole sky."

"I know where you mean. Are you thinking tonight?"

"I'd rather take it easy here tonight after my walk."

"You're certainly welcome and then that means tomorrow night and the night after you'll be watching the meteor shower," muses Mateen.

"You sound like you have plans."

"No, no plans."

"Okay, Mateen," says Anoo, wondering for a second if he's intruding but then deciding everything is fine.

"What did you bring for dinner?" Mateen laughs.

"I did bring some food." Anoo chuckles, knowing the cabin is well stocked. "I brought fresh bread and vegetables for tonight and some fresh eggs and new potatoes for breakfast. I thought I'd stay and sleep on the hill during the day, so I brought some trail food too."

"That should last you to the day after tomorrow," says Mateen almost to himself and then louder, "I'll make soup for tonight. That will be perfect with fresh bread."

"That sounds good. Would you like to come with me?" asks Anoo, wondering again if Mateen isn't telling him something.

"No, no, I'll watch from here and I'm sure I won't last the night."

"Has anything interesting happened around here lately?"

"Nothing out of the ordinary. Sometimes I think I've seen everything there is to see around here twice. Then, I'll happen to look closer at the right time and see something new. Which causes me to want to learn about some new insect, for example. Or, I'll walk down a path and see a doe nursing a fawn. Certainly interesting, but nothing new. This time though, the light might be particularly nice or it might be twins competing to suckle. Tell me about the farm, how things are growing and what's going on in town."

Mateen and Anoo enjoy talking and sipping until the sun is starting to set. While Mateen prepares dinner Anoo enjoys the spring-fed shower. Afterward they move to the front porch, looking west, to eat and watch the sun set.

"What has been going on in your life, my young friend. I've heard about the farm and town. What about you?"

"I've been a little unsettled of late. I like farm life. Watching things grow. Tending both plants and animals. I enjoy visiting my friends in town. The comradery, closeness with some of the girls. But I'm not feeling entirely myself or whole."

"It's not your farm, it's your parents', and as you say the girls aren't lifelong. Let me remind you of my way of looking at things. You've heard this before, but please, indulge me."

"Okay, Mateen."

"I want to emphasize the advantages of a person intentionally choosing the value systems they evaluate the world around them through. The value systems used to interpret their perceptive feelings."

"As you and my parents have taught and encouraged me to do."

"Yes, and you've done a very good job and made a very good effort, in that direction. This will be a bit of an overview of why one makes the effort to apply that intent."

"Okay, what are you thinking?"

"The general idea is that intentionally choosing one's value systems in life, intentionally choosing the value systems one uses to interpret their perceptive feelings, will increase individual awareness, identity, and opportunity. As compared to an individual who reacts to life through their perceptive feelings."

"Because perceptive feelings by themselves are a reaction to something that has happened around the individual. Or an assessment of something the individual has done," says Anoo.

"That's right, and the way to make that process not a reaction is to intentionally choose the value systems one uses to interpret what has already happened around them or what that individual has already done. The process of individually choosing one's value systems is one of thoughtful trial and error. An individual can apply a value system and then decide it is wrong or not quite right or only right for a particular time in one's life."

"Then that person can change the value system that they intentionally applied in the first place," adds Anoo.

"That's right and that choice to change the intentionally applied value system will result in perspective. It will result in a broader base with which to interpret or evaluate other intentionally applied value systems later in life."

"Which, hopefully, will result in a process of learning, changing, and growing," says Anoo.

"And that process of growth should go on throughout life. Potentially to a point where individuals identify themselves with the process of learning, changing, and growing. Finding identity by how one reacts to life through perceptive feelings based on adopted value systems won't reach that place where an individual can shift their identity from self to process."

"What is the advantage to that?"

"Consider your own individual potential. Aligning yourself with an established structure will slow you down. It doesn't matter whether the structure is religious, economic, military, or any other. You as an individual can learn, change, and so grow, faster through individual responsibility than you can waiting or depending on an established structure to change."

"If I waited I'd be limiting my potential."

"You would be limiting your potential to learn, change, and grow, right here on this glorious earth with your phenomenal potential. During this all too short of an opportunity to live your life that you have in front of you, right now, physically on this earth."

"I have been trying to do that and yet I feel like I can do more."

"That's not a statement of your own failings or lack of effort. The trying itself can create opportunities to do more. Sometimes the desire to do something different builds up over time. You've learned, changed, grown, and now you need a different base from which to try again, to try more."

"What is that different base?"

"Specifically, for you as an individual, I don't know. I only know it is an opportunity in front of you."

The rest of the evening is spent with some quiet reflection and casual conversation. The following morning starts with cool air and clear skies. The coolness won't last long, so Mateen and Anoo go for a walk along the little stream that runs in front of the cabin. They see a beaver swimming across a pond and a doe and fawn walk away from another pond after getting a drink. They stop and watch a small pond with good-size mayflies leaving the water and brookies looking for a meal. After five minutes, they continue walking after seeing two different brookies jump completely out of the water trying to catch a mayfly. One was successful; the other wasn't.

"How incredible the brookies' eye and body coordination must be to see the insect from underwater and catch it in the air," says Anoo.

"They see the insect and put themselves into the air, often close enough to catch the insect, despite the refraction of water and then the shift in perspective from looking through water to looking through air. All that is done as the insect is flying," agrees Mateen. "Some animal behaviors I can watch over and over again."

"They look like nice fat fish," comments Anoo.

"I eat some of them. That helps keep the population down and so their size up."

"There's more food for each individual," concludes Anoo.

"Yes, and the fish are cold-blooded, the water is relatively warm, and the prey is good-sized. That's why this time of year even with the relatively low success rate and high energy expenditure for catching the insects out of the air they catch enough for good growth now."

"I think they're hunting that way because it's fun. Summertime and the living is good." Anoo smiles.

"It's sure different for these guys when they have an ice roof over their heads," agrees Mateen and then, "Let's go back to the cabin before we disturb that family of mallards."

The sun is barely over the ridge when they get back and so is shining full on Mateen's east-facing back porch. They choose to go to the front porch with its morning shade. Looking west they see the aspen stand rising gently in front of them. Mateen has thinned out the undergrowth near the cabin. Farther away small shrubs mixed with a myriad of forbs and grasses thrive in the shade.

"What philosophizing have you been doing, my young friend?"

"Well, I've been thinking about how fanaticism is based on restricting one's information and how that can result in clarity. Clarity is something that people who are seeking an independent perspective are also seeking."

"The fanatic is basing their clarity on a less informed and narrower base than the person seeking an independent perspective."

"Wouldn't the clarity feel the same? Or, does the feeling of clarity change when the base of information it's based on is broader?" asks Anoo.

"That's a good question," says Mateen. "I'm thinking the fanatic's clarity is static and the base their clarity is on is static. The person seeking clarity from an independent perspective is constantly changing the base their desired clarity is on through the growth of learning. I guess I'm saying the feeling of clarity doesn't change for the fanatic or for someone seeking an independent perspective. It's the awareness of the breadth of the structure their clarity is based on that changes for the person seeking an independent perspective."

"So, the feeling of clarity doesn't change for the fanatic and their base doesn't change either because of their own restrictions to new learning. The process of learning, changing, and growing does cause a temporary loss of clarity for the seeker of an independent perspective. Familiarity and confidence in the process of learning, changing, and growing allows the seeker to go past that temporary loss of clarity inherent in learning something new to a broader base to perceive clearly from."

"That's good thinking, Anoo. Intentionally narrowing one's perspective to achieve clarity is a shortcut that fanatics use. Creating a broad base for clarity to sit on is a real effort. I tend to think that effort is rewarded by greater perspective."

"Perspective that allows for applying the same concept to beliefs, for example. The broader the base of learning one's beliefs sit on, the less superstition in those beliefs," concludes Anoo.

"Well done, my young friend. I would say there are two options for people in this physical realm. Not good or evil but the choice to be a follower or to be a creator."

"A creator of one's own perspective?" asks Anoo.

"Yes, I prefer the freedom of creating my own perspective. I do that by intentionally determining the value systems I use to interpret the world around me."

"As compared to a follower adopting an existing structure of value systems," says Anoo.

"No matter who or what one chooses, and so intends, to follow, that path is limited by who or what is being followed. I think the choice to create one's own independent perspective is limitless."

"Creating freedom for the individual," finishes Anoo.

"That's right! Learning about, changing, and growing the value systems you use to interpret the world around you is the process for determining your own independent perspective, thus creating individual freedom. I would say an individual's beliefs need to be tempered by what the individual knows or they will become a follower and superstitious."

"You're saying the independent individual's beliefs can reach out past their knowledge but shouldn't reach out so far superstition becomes incorporated into perspective. To put it another way—beliefs can legitimately reach out into ignorance from a place of knowing through experience. It is advantageous though, to be able to identify where knowledge ends and ignorance begins, to keep superstition out of perspective."

"That's right! I think followers use established structures to reach out beyond their own knowledge, which opens them up to other's errors and superstition. So I'm saying learn, learn, and learn some more. And you will change and grow because learning new things incorporates change and growth in the process."

"Okay, and the way to learn new things is to wonder, and ponder, and ask questions," says Anoo. "So, how does an individual start the whole process of wanting to know more?"

"Look out in front of you right now to the beauty that is around us all every day. Look at a blossoming flower. What is its name? Why does it bloom when it does? Learning doesn't take away from beauty. Look at a sunrise. Wonder why the colors are as they are. Quietly enjoy the colors. There's a time for learning and a time for contemplation. Feel the beauty in a compassionate gesture of an individual towards one less fortunate. Be the one that makes that gesture. As an individual, use that beauty to create in yourself the desire to forge your own independent perspective."

After contemplating the view for a few minutes Mateen says:

"What are your plans for the day?"

"I think I'll hang around through dinner and then walk to the hill in the evening. Then I'll stay two nights and come back here after sleeping in."

"That sounds good. Do you want some exercise today?"

"Sure, what do you have in mind?"

"I need to start getting my winter wood supply together."

Chapter Two

"HELLO, GRANDFATHER."

"Oh, hello, Laurel."

"Your mind was a long way away. You didn't even hear me walk up. You always know who's around you."

"I was off in my head thinking my own thoughts."

"You are always aware of what's going on around you even when you're thinking your own thoughts. Is everything all right?"

"Yes, I'm fine. I guess I was asleep."

"You are always aware of what's going on around you even when you're asleep, but, okay, if you say you're fine."

"Let's go for a walk, Granddaughter."

"I love our walks together—where to, anywhere in particular?"

"I want to go to a place nearby that has good memories for me."

"What memories?"

"You'll see, it's not far."

"Okay."

They walk across the large meadow their camp is in to the edge of the aspen stand that rings the top of the meadow. Turning around they look back toward camp. There are a few people active but most are relaxing in the heat of this hot August afternoon. The camp itself is toward the top of the meadow. A couple of horses are hobbled near camp.

Below that is a large area trampled and eaten down where their sheep spend the night. During the day the shepherds and their dogs move the sheep to other meadows to graze. At this point in the summer they're probably two or three miles away. At this time of day they're probably starting to graze their way back to camp for the night. Below the trampled area are scattered willows running along a small stream. As they turn and continue walking they enter the shade of the aspen stand. They climb through the stand to the top of a long ridge. The ground is rockier and the trees thinner as they walk along the game trail at the top of the ridge. After several miles the ridge ends in a rocky meadow above a steep, narrow valley. On the other side, a few hundred yards away, is a rocky hill a little higher than the ridge they're on.

"What is your favorite flower, Granddaughter?"

"I have too many favorites to pick one. Whichever ones are blooming at my feet are my favorite," she says, smiling.

"That's a good perspective but please indulge me and pick one."

"Okay, I'll go with the pyrola I most often see in the spruce-fir stands. They are so delicate and detailed, they always impress me."

"That's a good choice. My favorite is the red and yellow columbine. It was your grandmother's and my favorite. I came up here and picked some for her before walking down to camp and asking her to join her life with mine."

"I am delighted for us all that she said yes. Are you missing her more than usual?"

"I am and I guess I was hoping to find a columbine flower to remind me of her. I think it's a little late in the summer though, as I don't see any. Maybe there's a cool, damp spot around here where there is still one blooming. I guess right now I would like to sit and reminisce. Would you mind finding your way home from here?"

"Not at all. But would you rather I stayed? I can move off and wait. It's no trouble."

"That's okay. You find your way home. I'll be along for dinner."

"I hope your memories bring peace to you, Grandfather."

"Peace to you, Granddaughter."

At camp Laurel helps with the evening meal. She notes her grandfather getting back to camp safely and brings him dinner. After eating, everyone sits around their fires until they decide to sleep.

Anoo walks the half-dozen miles to the hilltop. There's a fair amount of up and down along the way. Overall, not a strenuous hike for him. Looking around and finding no cause for concern, he clears out a rocky area so that only gravel remains and makes a shallow depression for his butt and one for his heels. He lays out his sleeping bag with his feet roughly toward the east. At first he doesn't lie down but moves off to a spot where he can look for animals moving around in the evening light. Seeing not much in particular he lies down and naps. When he awakes the sky is dark. The moon has set behind the ridge to the west and the few cumulus clouds that were around in the afternoon have dissipated. After a couple of minutes he sees his first meteor. Not big, but it came quick and so is promising for a good show tonight. After seeing many dozens of shooters big and small he goes to sleep. In the early morning hours he wakes to the sound of coyotes. It is not the howling before and after a hunt, which is too common a sound to wake him. This is the sound of coyotes in active pursuit. He can hear their excited yipping as they keep track of each other in a full run down the ridge to his west. He can visualize that east-facing slope and its trees. He can see in his mind the panicked young deer separated from its mother. He can audibly hear the breaking of branches. He hears a last frightened bleat and then feels the silence that follows. He knows about the state of shock prey fall into when taken by a predator. He knows from placing his hand on the still beating chest of animals he has killed that this young deer's spirit is running through the trees with delightful abandon. Drinking deep from the cool waters of a clear mountain stream, savoring the taste of dew-coated greens. He falls back to sleep thinking of the lives of predator and prey. When he wakes the sun is up but not quite on him. He realizes he doesn't want to be up on the rocky hilltop through a hot August day. Dropping down the east side of the hill he enters an aspen stand, eats some trail food, and sleeps until noon.

The next day's camp business takes up half of Laurel's morning and then she relaxes. After a nice break, she wonders where her grandfather is. It's getting hot, so she goes to bathe in the stream with her two girlfriends. The water is shallow but there are a couple of pools deep enough to paddle around in and soak. When she gets back she still doesn't see her grandfather. Thinking shade, she looks for him in the aspens above camp.

"Hello, Grandfather."

"Hello, my Laurel."

"You look sad again. Are you thinking of Grandmother?"

"I was. Summer camp was a favorite place of ours. The only thing that could make summer camp better for us was you."

"And Mother also?"

"Yes, but grandchildren are easier favorites to have than children."

"Thank you for saying I'm a favorite. You are love in my heart and a joy to see every day."

"And you to me, Laurel."

"I wish there was something I could do to lift your spirits."

"You already have. I'm going to take a nap back at camp. Enjoy the coolness of these beautiful trees, my beautiful flower."

After sitting for a few minutes Laurel gets up and walks along the rocky ridge she walked the day before, thinking of red and yellow columbines and what she'll do for her grandfather. She gets to the end of the ridge again and looks over at the rocky hill above and across the narrow valley. She decides to stay on her side of the valley and moves to the northeast. To the coolest side of the ridge she's on. She drops down a little bit and stops and looks around. As she does she hears a drip. Looking between two large boulders, she sees a mossy depression and just below a glint of color. Yes! Mixed within green leaves fed from above by cool water are some of Grandfather's red and yellow columbines. They're past peak but still have good color. As she looks at them she suddenly turns and looks across the valley to an aspen grove. She knows someone has seen her. No one from camp should be here, and she saw her grandfather heading back to camp for a nap earlier. She can't see anyone and, thinking the person is hiding, prepares to run back up the hill. While regretting leaving the flowers she turns and takes a step up the hill. A man steps out from under the aspen trees across the valley and stops in the open. She continues uphill watching the man. He stays where he is. She gets to the top of the hill. Now, if he comes toward her, he will have to drop down, cross the bottom of the valley, and come uphill. She just needs to run along the top of the relatively flat ridge to stay away from him. Okay, she stops and looks at him. He waves and stays where he is. What to do? She waves and stays where she is. He sits down. That's encouraging. She stays where she is and sees him bring his hands to his mouth. Is he saying he's hungry? No, it just takes a second for his call to reach her.

"Hello, peace to you."

She waves again but doesn't say anything.

"My name is Anoo. Are you lost? I'm not. May I be of some assistance?"

His name is what?

"I'm fine. My name is Laurel."

She chooses to sit.

"I was napping in these aspens when I realized you were there.

I don't mean to intrude but I thought it would be more polite if I showed myself," says Anoo.

Okay, intruding is better than remaining unseen but he must have known she became aware of him before he showed himself. *I still need to be cautious and keep the advantage of the high ground,* she thinks. "What did you say your name was?"

"Anoo. My parents said their lives started anew when I was born."

"Is it spelled anew?"

"It's A-n-o-o. A little silly, I know."

"I like the sentiment."

"Laurel is a nice name. I've seen pictures of the flowers. They're beautiful."

"My grandfather says I was named Laurel to be his beautiful flower."

"I like the sentiment." After a few seconds Anoo says, "I spent the night up on the hill watching the meteor shower. What brings you out here, Laurel?"

"I'm looking for a gift for my grandfather. I was hoping to find some red and yellow columbines."

"There might be some around, but it's a little late. Maybe you'll beat the odds."

"Maybe so," she says, wishing she'd had time to pick the ones below. "Did you see many shooting stars?"

"Quite a few—it was a clear night and the timing is good. I should see just as many tonight."

"So, you'll stay here another night and then where to?"

"I'm staying with my great-uncle. His cabin is about six miles northwest of here. I'll stay with him a couple more days and then go back home. What about you? Where are you staying?"

Maybe I shouldn't tell him where I'm staying. But if I do he'll know my people are not far away.

"Camp is just along the ridge southeast of here. We bring our sheep up here every summer."

"Every summer? Why haven't I seen you before? I come up to the cabin a half-dozen times a year and into the valleys a couple times a year."

"Into the valleys, that's why—we stay east of the big valleys in the lower hills."

"Where do you winter?"

"We winter on the plains about sixty miles from here. What about you?"

"My parents' farm. It's a day's walk north of here. Would it be okay if I come closer? Yelling will make me hoarse."

"Okay. Will you please stay on your side of the valley?"

"Sure, I understand."

Anoo grabs his pack from in the aspens while Laurel checks her escape route along the ridge. She moves a little for a more direct path along the ridge and away from the valley. Anoo moves down closer to her. Then he looks around and sits on a little gravel spot. He takes his water bottle out and drinks. Then he reaches back into his pack and pulls out his binoculars.

"Would you mind if I look at you for a few seconds? I want to see you closer."

"I'm going to say I do mind. I don't have my monocular with me, so let's keep things even. Is that okay?"

"Yes, that's fine. Do you prefer a monocular to binos?"

"It's light and compact and so good enough. From what I've heard and your description there should be a town near your parents' farm."

"That's right. That's where I went to school."

"Do you work there too?"

"I work on my parents' farm about five miles downriver from town."

"What do you grow?"

"A wide variety of things. Corn, wheat, there's an orchard, a couple berry patches, row crops, pasture land, and a hay meadow. That's mostly where my father and I work. My mother concentrates on herbs, spices, and medicinal plants in the beds near the house. Where did you go to school? Or do go? How old are you?"

"I'm twenty-three and I went to school in the spring and fall when we went to town. For several winters I stayed in town for school also. That was some time ago. We have a small library at our place and our own classes at times. I'm more often teacher than student these days. How old are you?"

"I'm twenty-one. How far is your town?"

"Another sixty miles past our place. When we go to town we usually stay for a few weeks. School-age kids often stay longer."

"What's your place?"

"It's a group of cabins and barns next to a little stream with cottonwoods and a plum patch."

"Does everyone come into the hills with the sheep in the summer?"

"A half-dozen people always stay to keep an eye on things. Our goats don't summer up here so someone must stay with them. They also tend the gardens while we're away. In the spring we take wool to town and in the fall the sheep and goats that we're not going to winter. I imagine you sell your produce in town?"

"Yes, and we barter with neighbors for dairy products and calves and piglets."

"Do you have brothers and sisters or kids?"

"Just me. How about you?"

"The same. My mother is at winter camp. My grandfather is up here with me. I haven't had kids yet but would like to."

"In time, I see myself in a similar situation as my parents including kids. You came out here from camp by yourself. You're comfortable walking around the woods by yourself?"

"Yes, when I don't bump into strangers."

"I'm strange but not a danger."

"Why are you strange?"

"I don't think I am. I was just playing with words."

"Are you comfortable spending nights alone out here? I guess you must be."

"I am. I have a pistol in my pack and a walking staff. I have my feet and my senses. I'm not concerned."

"You have an impressive level of confidence. Or is it foolishness?"

"I certainly hope confidence. I first came out here on my own seven years ago with my uncle."

"You came out here on your own with your uncle or great-uncle?"

"I guess that didn't make much sense. He's my great-uncle but I shorten it to uncle usually. I came out here with him for a walkabout and at the end of our trip he headed for home and I stayed out for a few more days."

"Thank you for explaining."

"I've learned a lot about the place since then. I guess not as much as I could have because I haven't seen you guys before."

"We start moving the sheep in this direction around the middle of June. It usually takes a couple of weeks. We usually head back the end of September or so."

"My uncle comes to our place to help with spring planting in April. After he goes back I visit him a few times during the summer when the farm work is slow. Sometimes I just stay at his place. Other times I go in further but I'm usually between the valleys. Uncle comes down for harvest from roughly early September to mid-October and then we all go to his cabin for a fall hunt. You'd be gone by that time."

"What do you hunt?"

"We like to take a couple elk a year from up here. We also take a couple deer every fall from around the farm. Throw in a couple steers and a few pigs and we have enough meat for a year for all four of us and enough to take to town for sale."

"Do you hunt with your pistol?"

"I have but usually I use a bow and arrow."

"Where did you get your bow?"

"There's a guy in town who makes them and arrows. Another guy knaps the arrowheads."

"You don't use metal arrowheads?"

"I could have them made but I prefer the traditional stone."

"You must have to get close for a clean kill."

"That's right. I don't like to shoot from farther away than thirty yards. I prefer the challenge of getting close no matter what weapon I'm using. I still hunt and my goal is one shot, one kill," Anoo says with the confidence of experience.

"What is still hunting?"

"I sneak through the woods and try to beat the animals at their own game."

"That shows respect for the animals. I like that," says Laurel.

"They deserve the respect. I couldn't take a life any other way."

Laurel watches Anoo as he sits quietly. She knows he is thinking of the animals he has killed. Animals whose lives have sustained his life. Animals who, in some way, still live inside him. After a respectful period, she asks, "Have you ever used your pistol to protect yourself?"

"I've fired warning shots a few times. Only to make noise, not to try to harm. Sometimes the darkness of night makes normally wary animals bold."

"Tell me about a time you were concerned enough to fire warning shots," says Laurel.

"Most of the times were when I was camping by myself with a fire going at night. More people in camp keeps animals away, plus it's more likely there's a dog in camp. The dogs go on alert before the animals get close. Alone, I've had coyotes and bears nose around just outside the light. My shooting was just to get them to go away so I could go to sleep. The most interesting time was near the farm and during the day. The night before I had heard wolves howl. They usually stay up in these hills but sometimes in the winter they come down. I went across the river to see if I could find their tracks. There was only three to twelve inches of windblown snow on the ground so I walked instead of skied. I went out a few miles and found their tracks. I followed them for a mile until I saw where they had kicked up a deer. They chased the deer for a couple miles and that's where I saw them. They were hanging around the carcass after eating."

"How many were there?"

"Five. I watched for a little while and they became aware of me. I thought they'd stay by the carcass. I never got closer than a quarter mile. Surprisingly to me, they got up one by one and headed toward me. I moved away heading back to the river. They kept their distance for more than a mile and then started coming closer. It took them a little while to really get close. I was still several miles away from the safety of the river when I had to drop down into a gully. They ended up above me and only a hundred yards away. They had split up into two groups, one on either side of me."

"Let me interrupt. Why is the river safety and not your farm?"

"Downriver from town, where we are, all the people are on the west side of the river. I was on the east. Crossing the river means getting to the people side."

"Why are all the people on the west side of the river?" asks Laurel.

"There's some people on the east side near town. Where we are it's about five miles by a pretty straight road to town. There's a ridge to the west of the road and the river is on the east side. The ridge starts by town and runs out on the plains for about six miles. It's almost a thousand feet high by town and at its end it's still several hundred feet high before dropping off steeply and ending. The ridge faces east on our side so it isn't as dry as the west-facing side. Plus, the prevailing winter winds out of the northwest pile a bunch of snow towards the top of the ridge on the east side."

"Like a snow fence. We have snow fences to cause drifting."

"That's right. The east side of the ridge is tall shrub habitat, the west side mostly short grass and sagebrush. Gullies on the east side are lined with cottonwoods and some willows fed by the water running down from the melting snowdrifts."

"That makes for good people and animal habitat. Go on," Laurel encourages him.

"We're on the river side of the road. The road is a little above the river."

"So crossing the river means people and dogs nearby. Okay, back to the story, you had wolves above you and were still a few miles from the river."

"Yes, when one of the wolves started dropping down into the

gully I was in, I turned around and shot three times between the two groups of wolves."

"Three being a distress signal. What did the wolves do?"

"They all went out of sight behind the hill where I had just been. A few minutes later I reached the top of the hill on the other side. I looked behind me and saw the wolves on the far side. I looked ahead and saw horses coming a couple miles away."

"Who was it?"

"My father had become concerned for me. He had saddled up our two horses so I could ride back and with one of our dogs he went to the downstream neighbors. He went there first because they have two boys fifteen and twelve I often hike around with."

"How old were you?"

"Sixteen. When my father got there the boys were there so not out with me. Their father was there also. They all saddled up and brought one of their dogs to help look for me. Everyone had heard the wolves the night before so they headed in that direction."

"They thought that was the most likely direction you'd gone with you being you," Laurel says with assurance.

"That's right. They crossed the river and went to the top of a little hill to look around. They were talking about splitting up into pairs to look for my tracks when they heard my shots. It only took them a few minutes to get to me on horseback. They saw the wolves as they rode up. The boys followed the tracks back to the deer carcass, where the wolves had stopped and stood their ground. They left them alone and rode back."

"Leaving you with a story to tell. Did you get in any trouble at home?"

"Not really. It was explained to me that I should always say where I'm going because even little walks can turn into long hikes."

"You being you and all. What would you have done if they weren't looking for you?"

"If the wolves had gotten close enough I could have shot one. They're smart animals. They'd have kept their distance after that and would remember seeing one of theirs killed by a person for the rest of their lives."

"Still, it must have been nice to see the horses coming towards you."

"It very much was and to ride back with everyone. Okay, now tell me more about you. How many sheep and goats do you guys have?"

"It's not quite as exciting but we have about three hundred sheep now and we winter around two hundred usually. That gives us plenty to eat and sell in town. We winter around a hundred goats. In the spring after taking wagon loads of wool to town we still have plenty to spin and weave."

"I like the colors of your shawl."

"Thank you. It's cashmere and light enough to be comfortable keeping the sun off on a hot afternoon and still good for cool mornings. I see colors on your shirt."

"My mother sews and embroiders. She's the decorative one."

"Only the practical for you?"

"Pretty much, I guess."

"Any artwork of any kind?"

"I like to drum and I..."

"Oh come on, tell me."

"Well, I have to admit I like to make dried floral arrangements in the fall. I make a couple for the house and I give a few to friends and neighbors."

"You're such a rough and tough mountain man."

"Usually I only eat raw liver but I do bathe twice a year whether I need to or not."

"In that case it's nice talking from a distance like this, isn't it?"

"Ha ha, good one, Laurel. I would like to be closer to you. I like talking to you."

"I like talking to you too. But let's keep some distance. Not because I'm concerned you smell."

"Okay, how long can you stay?"

"A little longer if you'd like. Did you come up here to be alone?"

"No, it just didn't occur to me to ask anyone. I spent the night with friends in town before I came up here. I knew they had to work these next couple days. Do you want to look for columbines for your grandfather?"

"I actually just saw some when I felt you looking at me."

"Would you like to pick some? I'd like to talk some more."

"I'd like that too. Do you have a girlfriend in town?"

"No one that I have future plans with. What about you?"

"The same. Going to town always has a social side to it for us."

"Are you interested in a life in town or do you prefer the variety of seasonal movements?" asks Anoo.

"At this point I prefer the seasonal movements. Different circumstances could point toward a different future though. Are you thinking you'll always be a farmer on your parents' farm? Bring some lucky girl into your family?"

"That's a possibility. Maybe I'll start my own farm nearby, or maybe I'll explore new places like settlements out on the plains."

"Do you have sheep on the farm?"

"Not sheep. We have horses, cows, pigs, turkeys, chickens, dogs, and cats. How about you guys?"

"Sheep, goats, horses, chickens, dogs, and cats."

"So, no pigs or turkeys. How much trouble do you guys have with predators?"

"Some, even though there are always people, dogs, and horses near the sheep. We end up with some coyote furs for winter coats and a bearskin rug every year. The fur isn't as thick as in the fall but it's thick enough."

"Do you hunt too or are the sheep, goats, and chickens your main sources of meat?"

"I don't go out on the hunts but we always get some antelope in the fall from around winter camp and every other year or so we get a bison or two. Some guys stay up here after everyone else leaves in the fall and they take some deer and elk."

"Why don't you take bison every year?"

"Some years we don't see any. When they do come around we usually take more than one. There doesn't seem to be enough to try harder to take more."

"What vegetables do you grow?" asks Anoo. "You said the people who don't come up here with the sheep tend gardens. We grow many kinds and are our own seed source for all we grow."

"We have the basics. I bet you guys have more."

"If you know what you'd like I could go home and get you some seeds."

"You'd go all the way home and back again just to bring us some seeds for planting next spring? Why would you do that?"

"To make a gesture towards you and your people. A gift because you interest me."

"Why do I interest you?"

"Because you're here and I'm enjoying your company. I only expected to see my uncle and some shooting stars. I had no idea I'd meet a woman out here. Your lifestyle intrigues me."

"My lifestyle intrigues you?"

"Well, yes, the seasonality of your people's movements intrigues me. Mostly though, it's you who intrigues me. We're roughly the same age and I'm interested."

"I'm enjoying our conversation and I'm interested in you too. We have a couple days to get to know each other. Let's do that instead of your racing home and back for some seeds."

"Does that mean you'd come back tomorrow, Laurel? I'd like that very much."

"I'd like it too and yes, I will. I still have some time today. I know a little about where and how you live and who you live with. Tell me more."

"Like day-to-day stuff?"

"Start with ceremonies or celebrations."

"Well, there's the solstices and equinoxes, birthdays and anniversaries."

"What about weddings?"

"My parents were married by my uncle. That's the last wedding in the family."

"Is your uncle the leader of a church? How could that be since he lives in the hills and it seems by himself since you haven't mentioned anyone else?"

"He does live by himself and he wouldn't belong to a church. He's a religious independent. He married my parents by being a witness to their pledge to share their lives with each other."

"How does that constitute a marriage?"

"I would say it's a marriage between two people who don't recognize religious authority, only responsibility for their own actions."

"Are you a religious independent?"

"Yes, what about you? Any particular grouping or direction of interest?"

"Direction of interest, yes. I'd say I'm an independent also. No group has influence over me. Only my own people and that's through information and perspective, not a religious structure. Tell me about your religious independence."

"I would say that I am responsible for my own religious perspective. I can be inspired by a book or another person but only to add to my own perspective. So, there's individual perspective, not dogma. There are prophets but not saviors. Accuracy in perspective is based on explanation, not the title or position of who is talking."

"We could spend a day talking about any one of those statements, Anoo. But they're not religious from a supreme deity standpoint. What about a creator or a great spirit?"

"We're in a universe and it had to come from somewhere. I think the universe started when something identified itself as a being."

"Out of nothing comes a realization, a realization of I am I. A realization of identity that a being we call the God of the universe somehow found," states Laurel. "That would be the singularity that is the source of the big bang and so the universe. You don't go along with the idea that the universe has always existed?"

"I like the perspective of beginning through the intent of a creator, but I certainly wouldn't say I know for sure."

"Okay, please continue," Laurel encourages.

"That was some fifteen billion years ago. Since then, that being has seen thousands and thousands of intelligent species come and go to extinction and trillions and trillions of intelligent individuals come and go."

"So 'that being' didn't study geology and astrophysics for billions of years before producing its crowning achievement of humanity here on Earth as an egocentric perspective would suggest?"

"I agree, Laurel, and well said. I do think the earth revolves around the sun."

"Meaning the solar system isn't centered on humanity let alone the universe. I agree, I think it's our perceptions and our perspective that we are each the center of. That can be fact and not extrapolate out to humanity and the universe. It doesn't matter how many people feel they're the center of the universe. That perspective is still a perspective and can be in error."

"Quality trumps quantity," adds Anoo.

"One cannot petition God with prayer," agrees Laurel.

"One thought where 'the light goes on' has more value than a million idle thoughts," Anoo says, continuing the concept.

"Multiplying by zero will always get you nothing," says Laurel.

"I'd rather make my own mistakes than follow someone else's imperfect path. You are an interesting person, Laurel, but I need a quick break."

"Me too and I'd like to pick a couple flowers for my grandfather. Can we meet back here in a few minutes?"

"Sure. How are we going to do that and yet have you feel safe?"

"I guess I'm just going to have to trust you, Mister Pistol in His Pack."

"Peace to you, Laurel."

"And to you, Anoo."

Anoo and Laurel walk out of sight of each other for their break. Before coming back out in the open Anoo finds himself washing his face while similarly Laurel adjusts her shawl and hair. Sniffing his armpits Anoo decides a little distance is a good thing. Laurel drops down the hill to pick a few of the freshest red and yellow columbine flowers and wraps them in a cashmere handkerchief with some wet moss. Climbing back up she looks for Anoo.

"Hello, Laurel, it's nice to see you again," Anoo says, laughing.

"And you, Anoo. I like our chance meeting and your company is pleasant on this pleasant day."

"Thank you. I'm enjoying our conversation. Would you like to continue?"

"I think I'll head back to camp."

"I was hoping you'd stay longer but you said you'd come back tomorrow. I'd like that very much, please do."

"I will. Otherwise I wouldn't want our conversation to end either. What time do you think? Would you like me to bring you anything?"

"I'm good for another day. Thank you for offering. How about around noon so I can get some sleep?"

"Okay. Will you watch all night?"

"Maybe, it depends on how good a show it is. Will you watch for a while too? Let's both watch together but apart."

"Okay, I'll watch but I won't guarantee for long. I'll be back around noon to tell you what I see."

"I look forward to our next meeting, Laurel."

"And I also, Anoo."

They both stand and stretch for a minute. Then with a wave Anoo turns and bounds up the hill from rock to rock not missing a step and covering fifty yards uphill in a dozen seconds. Laurel realizes he could have come toward her at any time. If she had started running down the trail along the ridge he would have reached the top of her side of the hill much faster than she thought. She didn't want to think past that, and that isn't what he did. He showed her what he could have done. Now he has stopped and is looking at her. Their eyes connect across the valley and it's as if the distance between them has gone away and they are within arm's reach. After a minute, they both break eye contact and then see each other from across the valley again. Anoo reaches his arm above his head and gives a big wave. She waves back. He turns and steps into the aspen and is gone from sight.

She turns, walks a bit, and starts to run. She feels her hair out behind her and her feet hitting the ground. Then she feels her arms pumping and the breath going in and out of her lungs. Now she is in her head and looking out in front. She is going so fast she can't look down to where her feet are. She is looking three and four steps ahead, picking the spots where her feet will land next. Skimming the ground, her feet unerringly find the now unseen spots she has picked. Looking a couple of extra steps ahead she shifts her stride by half a step and puts her pushing off foot just in front of a downed log. She sails over it and lands on the other side with her foot finding the spot she could only see for an instant as she leapt. Looking ahead again she races soundlessly along the ridge. Dipping her head and reaching out with her arms she fends off branches without missing a step. She races by a pine squirrel on the ground and only five feet away. It stares unmoving until feeling the mass of her go by then runs up a tree to a low branch where it looks at her without chattering, as silent as she. Getting to the ridge above camp she slows to a walk and catches her breath.

As she steps out into the open and spots camp, she sees the valley and her people with familiarity and detachment. Something has changed. She looks over and sees her grandfather sitting down and looking at her. He smiles and waves. How much does he know of her afternoon? He's too polite for details but she knows he keeps an overview of her when she's out of sight. She can always feel his presence if she tries. He knows more than he shows. She walks up to him, opens her handkerchief, and shows him her columbines. Overcome with emotion he lowers his head. She lets the flowers fall from her hands on to him and they bounce into his lap. She goes behind him and to the side a few steps and sits as he looks at the flowers. Dinnertime comes and she helps him up and they walk to their meal hand in hand.

Anoo relaxes in the aspen until the sun is setting and the hilltop is out of direct sun. He's napped again and is ready for another night of stargazing. As he eats trail food he is looking to where Laurel was sitting as they talked. She's interesting to talk to and has no qualms about walking alone in these hills. What an unexpected development. Is she thinking of him as he is her? Maybe, but she is in a camp of people while he is alone on a hilltop. What will tomorrow bring? Perhaps it's best to just enjoy the night's shower.

After full dark while stretched out on his bed Anoo watches the night sky and counts. At one point he sees six shooters in as many seconds and wonders if Laurel has seen them also. A satellite goes by, pulsating with light at one-second intervals as though it is slowly rotating. Without expecting to, or knowing why, he falls asleep.

Chapter Three

WAKING EARLY IN the morning Anoo eats and then suddenly puts on his pack and goes back to Mateen's cabin. His uncle isn't here. He's probably on an early morning nature walk. Anoo takes a shower and rinses out his shirt. After cleaning up he goes to the pantry and finds a packet of a variety of spices given to Mateen by his mother. He goes to the backyard, where Mateen has a rock pile of little treasures he's brought home over the years. He chooses a small piece of petrified wood that looks like a dried branch and has an interesting bark pattern. He sends a "peace to you" thought to Mateen and heads back to the rocky hill at a slow enough speed that he won't break a sweat. When he gets there he goes into the shade of an aspen stand and waits.

Laurel has risen early and taken an early morning bath before breakfast. She helps prepare the morning meal for camp and then cleans up after the herders leave to move the sheep. After cleanup she goes to her tent and looks around. She picks a small bone flute from her belongings. Deciding not to wait until noon she starts to walk up the hill. Turning, she sees her grandfather looking at her and waves. He smiles and waves. When she reaches the top of the ridge she slowly walks down the path she raced along yesterday. Taking her time, she smells the scents and listens to the sound of the aspen leaves rustling in the morning breeze. She notes fresh elk tracks crossing the ridge from one little draw and dropping down into another. She stops and watches and listens into the draw the elk went down. A half an hour later she starts walking again. She didn't see or hear any elk but feels calm and comfortable. She feels like she's in the moment. She's not thinking of camp nor of seeing Anoo again. She's just walking.

When she gets to the end of the ridge she stops and adjusts her clothes and hair. Then she wonders if she'll disturb Anoo's rest because she's a couple of hours early. She calls out and Anoo immediately steps out from the aspens and they look at each other across the distance. Like their parting yesterday their eyes meet and their perception of each other draws close together. After a minute Laurel shifts her eyes from his, breaking the connection. Anoo gestures to his side of the steep little valley and then to hers. Okay, enough with the distance. She gestures to her side and walks toward the rocks and the little seep where she picked the columbines the day before. She sits and looks over at Anoo. He starts to slowly walk up to her. As he nears she stills the little flutter of nervousness she's feeling. Is it because he's Anoo or because he's virtually a stranger? She stands and thinks, *A little of both*. Anoo stops about ten feet away and they look at each other. Then he steps forward and holds out his hand. She steps forward and holds out her hand. Looking each other in the eye they shake hands like a couple of gentlemen. Then she steps back and they sit about ten feet from each other.

"Did you see many shooting stars?" asks Laurel.

"I saw a lot even though I didn't stay up all night. Did you see any?"

"I saw some but I wasn't awake watching for long."

"You look very nice. Is that the same shawl as yesterday?"

"Thank you, it is."

"I can see it with more detail today. The colors and the pattern work well together."

"Thank you. It's one of my favorites."

"Did you make it yourself?"

"I did. I enjoy the spinning and weaving and it's good sharing time with the girls. I must say you look fresher than I thought you would after a couple nights in the woods."

"I got up early this morning and went to my uncle's and cleaned up. He has a very refreshing spring-fed shower. I wanted to present myself well and feel comfortable around you today."

"I thank you, Anoo, I appreciate the effort. What was your uncle up to?"

"I didn't see him. He must have been off on one of his nature hikes. I'm sure he was up at first light and went wandering in the coolness of early morning. He probably knew I was there and knew there wasn't any reason to come back and see what was going on."

"I like your shirt. It looks like your mother puts a lot of detail into her embroidery."

"She does for her favorite projects. I like your hair. It's longer than I could tell yesterday. I like long braids."

"Thank you. How do you hold your ponytail back?"

"This is just a leather sleeve," says Anoo, turning his ponytail toward her. "I have some fancier hair ties but not with me."

"Did your mother do the beadwork on your moccasins too?"

"Yes, they were made in town and she decorated them."

"Do you prefer soft soles over hard?"

"For moving through the woods quietly soft soles are a must. I have heavy work boots for some uses but not the woods. I like to feel what's under my feet."

"Are you an accomplished stalker?" wonders Laurel.

"I like to think so. I like to observe wildlife behavior and there's no substitute for watching animals that don't know you're there and have no reason to expect that a person is nearby."

"That gives you the opportunity to watch them be themselves," comments Laurel and then says, "Tell me some of your best observations or stalks."

"The best ones to me usually involve an unexpected result after an unexpected choice."

"Hmm, please explain," encourages Laurel.

"I'll be moving through the woods keeping track of wind direction and keeping quiet and then for a reason unknown to me I will change direction and speed up or slow down and then I end up seeing something I had no idea was there."

"Do you think you smelled or heard something and it didn't fully consciously register with you?" suggests Laurel.

"At times I think that is what happens. With an animal for example. But I've done the same thing with rock specimens, so I don't think that is what is always happening."

"Give me an example of how that has happened with rock specimens."

"Well, it is like I said. I'll be looking for things."

Laurel interrupts him. "What kind of things?"

"Anything that would be of interest to me. It could be a rock specimen or a feather, or skull, or an unusual plant. I'll just be out sneaking around, trying to create as little disturbance as possible, and seeing what is out there. Then, suddenly, I change course, walk a little bit and there's a nice crystal or a nice piece of petrified wood. Something better than I've seen that day and that I couldn't see, smell, or hear."

"Give me a more specific example."

"I've looked at a hillside from a little distance and then walked up on it and stopped. I looked around and then down at my feet and I had stopped right in front of a small grouping of petrified wood pieces with a beautiful root beer color and wrapped in bark mineralized a shiny white. I went back to the same hill the next day with two friends and we searched the whole hill and didn't find another piece of even average petrified wood. Another time I was out wandering and ready to go back to camp. For some reason, I just kept on walking. I was tired and thirsty but just kept on going. Finally, I said, 'I'm stopping here. I am not going farther.' Then I…well…"

"You can't stop partway through your story," admonishes Laurel.

"Okay, I needed to pee. I had just started when I looked down at the ground and had to move to keep from peeing on a beautiful whole, white bird point."

"Wow! Okay, I've got the idea. How do you think you become aware of what you are moving towards when there's no sensorial input to become aware of? It's not like yesterday when I became aware you had seen me. I felt your attention, your concentration on me. My awareness of you was through a sixth sense. A feeling but not a skin sensation type of feeling. You had actively reached out to me."

"That's right. It isn't an awareness of something else that has awareness like looking a wild animal in the eye. Even if I'm completely hidden from the animal, if I make eye contact the animal will know I'm there. This is becoming aware of something that can't reach out to me."

"Come on, let's hear it. You've thought about this before."

"Yes, I have. I think I send my center of perception out away from myself."

"All right, I think I'm following but would you please develop that concept a little more, Anoo?"

"I think I can send my ability to perceive away from myself, on a sort of string of myself. I then perceive from the end of that string."

"It sounds like there is more than one self involved there."

"It's not an easy phenomenon to explain. I've sat quietly and perceived away from myself by thinking of where I want to send my perception. Then I kind of feel my perception move to that place. When I'm walking I think I do the same thing but I'm less aware I'm doing it. Because I'm concentrating on moving through the woods without disturbing what is around me. When I perceive something from the end of a string while I'm walking I think the information comes to me more as an impulse to go somewhere than a sensorial perception."

"I think that's a good explanation. It's similar to your attention reaching out to me yesterday but you actively perceive when you're out there at the end of a string. Do you think when you perceive from the end of a string you can hear, see, smell, and taste like when your ability to sense is in the body? I'll leave out the feeling of touch because you're saying you're away from your body. I guess I shouldn't include taste either."

"It's not the same. I'm seeing and hearing from the end of a string but the same clarity of perception isn't there. I think I end up perceiving something like a piece of petrified wood because it has been alive at one time and so is different from other rocks. I don't think I perceive its quality from the perspective of a rock hound, a person who loves to hunt for interesting rocks. On the other hand, I think I walk right by petrified wood that isn't of high quality and go toward pieces that are high quality."

"That sounds contradictory. But first, what's quality in a piece of petrified wood to a rock hound like you?"

"Well, I wanted to bring you a gift today to show how much I enjoyed talking to you yesterday. I brought you a piece of petrified wood."

"Is that because you expected this turn of conversation?"

"I can send my perception out on a string but not through time. My not being able to do so currently doesn't mean I consider it an impossibility. I do think nonlinear time is perceived through a different methodology though."

"Let's come back to nonlinear time in another conversation."

"Okay, here, let me throw you this piece of petrified wood."

"I thank you for your gift, Anoo. I appreciate the sentiment. I do have to critique your gift. That's because of our conversation and how the importance of quality in a piece of petrified wood to a rock hound fits in. I would never critique a gift otherwise."

"I understand, please go ahead," says Anoo.

After giving Laurel a minute to examine the piece of petrified wood Anoo begins his explanation.

"You can see the detail in the wood. The furls in the bark are very distinct. When you look at the end you can see the growth rings."

"It looks so much like a regular piece of wood I would most likely walk right by. I'm sure it takes experience for a rock hound to see what is special to them."

"It does take experience, and guidance from someone already

experienced is very helpful. Sometimes wood mineralizes like this and sometimes pieces end up with colors the wood itself never had. The details of this piece show because the mineral solution involved contained minute grains of quartz. The grains were so small they were dissolved in groundwater. Pieces of wood that are not as nice, from a rock hound's perspective, mineralize with coarser grains and/or drabber coloration."

"Okay, and so you're saying that you won't impulsively move towards a low-quality specimen?" encourages Laurel.

"I did say that, which you pointed out conflicts with the idea that perceiving from out on a string is different than perceiving directly through sensorial organs. Now I'm wondering if I do perceive things when I'm out there on a string with the same perspective, or value systems, I have when I'm directly sensing through my body. I guess it's still me out there after all."

"Perhaps you can perceive that the piece used to be alive more clearly when the piece itself has a quality that, coincidentally, is of quality to a rock hound. The specimen clearly showing as petrified wood in your hand somehow shows clearer from a distance that it was once alive. Maybe the process of perceiving out on a string only seems different because that process does not have the familiarity to you that the daylong use of body based sensorial perception does."

"Lack of familiarity," Anoo considers. "I do see and hear when I'm out on a string. But smell hasn't been there. Perhaps because, as you say, a lack of familiarity, not a lack of capability."

"Maybe even feeling on skin and ability to taste can go out with you on a string with more experience," suggests Laurel. "Like feeling wind when you're out there for example. Do you know how you would have sensed the bird point?"

"I think that is because of the intent that would have been applied to the stone when the knapper shaped it, leaving something perceivable behind."

"That seems similar to my sensing you when you became aware of me yesterday. I sensed your attention focused on me."

"You sensed me become aware of you. Did a string of me reach out to you? Did my mind reach out to you?"

"I felt your focused awareness of me in my mind," says Laurel.

"I certainly focused on you more than a flower I walked by for example. I focused my awareness through my sight on you. I saw you were female and relatively young. When I send out my perception on a string I think the string comes out of my solar plexus and then I perceive from there. I saw you but didn't perceive you from a position of being next to you. Is that two different things? One a mental connection and the other a body connection?" wonders Anoo.

"I guess I'm not sure," says Laurel. "On the one hand, you're perceiving from a physical position away from your body. Some sort of string, a string that is a part of you, carries your perceptive ability away from you. In the other case I became aware of you after you perceived me from your physical perspective. Wouldn't some part of you have to have reached out to me for that to happen? A string of you without your ability to perceive? I must have followed something, call it a string of you, for me to have been able to turn around and look right where you were."

"Still, is it a body connection or a mental connection? Is there really a difference? Those kind of connections are something I'm working on. Let's put that aside and come back to it later."

"We'll add it to the list of topics to come back to later, like nonlinear time," says Laurel.

"I'm a little surprised that you don't seem put off by the topic of perceiving out on a string away from the body," says Anoo.

"You took a chance opening yourself up with this topic and I appreciate that. I'll say I think I know what you mean because when I leave my body in a dream state I have a similar understanding. It isn't when I'm out there perceiving but when I want to return. If I happen to find myself in a situation I'm not comfortable with and I want to return to my body I intentionally try to move a part of my body like my finger or hand. That causes me to return. It feels like I'm being pulled back to myself, reeling myself back in until I'm moving so fast everything blurs."

"That sounds like there are a lot of selves involved," says Anoo with a smile.

"It is a hard topic to explain." Laurel laughs.

"Reeling a string back in?" asks Anoo.

"Pretty much, yes."

"I appreciate your sharing and I understand the similarities in methodologies of perceiving away from the body asleep or awake. I think dreams are remarkably interesting too. I need to stretch and regroup a little," says Anoo.

They stand up and move around. Shaking and stretching away their inactivity. At one point they both smile when they catch each other glancing out of the corner of their eyes at the other. After a few minutes they sit back down and continue their conversation.

"I'm enjoying our conversation, Anoo. The idea that people can send their ability to perceive away from themselves while awake in the physical is very interesting."

"And the idea that a person can do the same in a realized dream is interesting too," replies Anoo.

"By 'realized dream' you mean the person becomes aware that they are dreaming but doesn't wake up; they continue dreaming. So, who's who and what's what? Who sends what out on a string to perceive away from the body? What awakes when a dream is realized?" asks Laurel.

"I guess it can only be the individual in each case because there's no one else involved. The individual is the one who acts, the one who directs the actions, the one who becomes aware of their own actions. I'll say the individual starts out as an infant that can perceive. As the individual matures they learn to identify themselves more and more with what is doing the perceiving, not just what is being perceived."

"It sounds like your definition of maturing is the creation of perspective. You're saying that an infant starts out with an ability to perceive. As perceptions accumulate into childhood a framework is being created that will eventually be identified as the individual. I would say that framework is created through feelings about perceptions at first and later through thoughts about perceptions by reflection. Where do you think the framework is created?"

"I would say in the mind through thoughts," decides Anoo. "Feelings or perceptions influence the thoughts but do not house them."

"Does our perspective end when the mind ceases to function?" asks Laurel.

"I don't think so because I think there is a quality to thoughts and feelings that can be reached that creates soul. Soul being defined as the part of us that doesn't end with the death of the body. Perhaps the mind and body are designed to accumulate thoughts and feelings, of enough quality, into an organized energy that lasts beyond death."

Laurel considers this and then responds.

"An infant perceives, a child accumulates, a young adult considers and reflects, and so creates what an adult identifies as their individual perspective. Adults, having created their own individual perspective, can then learn to identify themselves as the process of creating perspective, not the process of perceiving. Perceiving is the raw material. With perspective, thoughts and feelings of enough quality can accumulate into an energy that lasts beyond death. Possibly that capability is one that has evolved over time. Or maybe humans were designed to do that. Wow! That is some independent thinking, Anoo. Well then, what value systems can a person hold to increase the possibility that they will have thoughts and feelings of enough quality that they add energy to their soul?"

"Good question. I'll start with the person's choice to determine their own value systems."

"Okay, first, you're saying you agree with the value system, that it is advantageous to an individual to determine their own value systems," Laurel says with a smile, "the value systems the individual uses to interpret the world around them. That's compared to adopting societal value systems or the value systems one ends up with by reacting to life through one's feelings. Either way those are value systems established through acceptance, not through the benefit of reflection."

"That's right, Laurel. The process of choosing one's own value systems raises a person's identity up from a victim who reacts to life through their feelings to an individual who acts through choice. That process of intentional choice creates an awareness that people who put the determining of their value systems into their subconscious can't reach. An awareness of why they act the way they do, an awareness that can be explained to others."

"You're saying the individual will become a completely different person by the end of their life if they hold their value systems by choice. As compared to who the same individual would become if they had left their value systems to their subconscious," states Laurel. "Okay, what are some examples?"

"People who keep their own value systems in their subconscious, where the values are not directly a choice, can end up interpreting the process of having a thought where 'the light goes on' as a revelation from God. People who are aware of their own value systems interpret a thought where the light goes on as a thought of unique value. I have decided to define that thought of unique value as a thought with enough power to create soul," concludes Anoo.

"Okay, so first you're saying it's a value system you hold that thoughts where the light goes on are your thoughts and not a revelation from God. Why did you make that choice?" asks Laurel.

"I've had thoughts where the light goes on and I'm the only one there. No hand of God came down from a brilliantly lit sky full of puffy white clouds with shafts of light streaming through them to extend a finger towards me and touch my forehead."

"I don't think that happens to the people who interpret thoughts like those as a revelation either." After thinking for a second Laurel continues, "Which is why you think there is interpretation going on which allows for the possibility of error in perspective. Interpretation by someone who already sees God acting in their lives, someone who wants to give responsibility for things in their life to God. So the difference in perspective is something being given by a superior being as compared to the individual accomplishment of having thoughts of a quality that can accumulate energy. Energy that, potentially, can continue after the death of the body. The difference between 'something has given me this' as compared to 'I have accomplished this,'" says Laurel. "Awareness creates quality."

"I think that over time those two different value systems, those two different interpretations of the same phenomenon will result in an individual profoundly different from who they might have been," states Anoo.

"One individual holding one value system will become a person with a different perspective than the same individual holding another value system throughout their life. That sounds like the future is not set; our fate is what we make," says Laurel.

"I think a reactionary value system results in vagueness. A lack of awareness and so a lack of capability. A lack of choice, so a lack of opportunity. Value systems developed with awareness create potential and opportunity, including the awareness to teach others," says Anoo.

"You're saying the process of determining one's own value systems results in a clarity that lends itself to the ability to communicate concepts to others. Thereby creating the opportunity to raise a person above the 'don't think—obey' of 'I'm right because I feel like it.' Or, the 'don't think—obey' of 'I'm right' because of my position in a hierarchy or because of my status. Giving someone the explanation of a concept and what it's based on, in other words proving one's point, allows the listener to evaluate the concept on their own. It gives the listener the opportunity to evaluate concepts through their own experiences and thoughts. Which can then make their perspective their responsibility. An independent perspective is one created by the individual. It can't just be the perspective an individual happens to have. They must create it themselves."

"That is incredibly well put, Laurel. I want to conclude with my own words also."

"Yes, please."

"An example of a thought that has potential to add energy to an individual's soul is a thought that grows perspective, not just a thought that accumulates information. A feeling with the same potential would be like the feeling of having done well after helping a needy person recover their health or dignity and be able to move on in life. It won't come from tossing a scrap to a beggar with disdain. It won't come from a person doing their job in a medical clinic in a robotic way. It comes from acting with clarity and intent in one's daily life."

"I think that's deep enough thinking to require a break," suggests Laurel. "Let's take a walk and see how our individual perspectives compare while observing the same phenomenon."

Walking up the rocky hill, choosing their own paths so they can walk side by side, they reach the top of the ridge. When the single-animal-wide trail along the top of the ridge starts Anoo gestures Laurel to go ahead. She walks a little way along the trail and turns east, downhill toward thicker aspen. The game trail she chooses drops down steeply at first. They sidestep down until they reach a bench with thick vegetation growing between tall aspen. It is a completely different habitat than the widely spaced and shorter aspen up on the rocky ridge. Laurel turns off the game trail and walks between the tree trunks through thigh-high forbs and grasses. She stops next to two trees that are growing so close together it is hard to distinguish through the vegetation growing near the ground if they are one tree or two. She wraps her arms around one trunk and looks at Anoo. He slowly looks around in all directions and sniffs the air. Satisfied they're safe, he steps up and hugs the other tree. They hold their embraces for an unknown time. Laurel slowly opens her eyes and sees Anoo open his with a faraway look in his eyes.

"Where did you go?" asks Laurel. "And please don't adjust your opinion because of a perceived reaction from me."

"When I first put my arms around the trunk my elbow brushed against your arm just above your elbow. My entire concentration jumped to the feel of your arm through our clothes. The give of your skin against my elbow became the awareness of all of you next to me."

"Okay, I felt that too, but that's not where I was pointing the conversation."

"I wasn't adjusting my opinion as you suggested," explained Anoo.

"I know. But keep going."

"I felt the bark as cool and smooth on my cheek with a powdery coating interspersed with rough sections of bark I felt against my arms. Then I felt my perception leave myself and go up the inner bark with the sap flowing from the roots up to the leaves. As I neared the leaves that are in the sun the sap and I quickened until I was in a warm green glow. After feeling my awareness in that glow for some amount of time I must have moved my cheek against the bark. Because I became aware of myself some sixty feet below and I slowly went back down to my body. What about you?"

"Pretty much the same. I very much enjoyed the experience. I guess this isn't an experience where our independent perspectives are very different. Let's do it again and see if we can perceive ourselves in each other's tree," suggests Laurel.

"Okay, let me look around again."

Anoo looks and sniffs again until he is comfortable. Laurel wonders why she doesn't feel the need to check her surroundings herself. She usually would. *Why do I feel so much comfort so soon with this man?* Then her perception is moving up the tree again.

"You first," says Anoo after several minutes.

"I wanted to turn and look at you but I think I ended up with my back to you as I looked out. As though the trees aren't concerned with each other. They look out from each other as though they are one tree. As though they have each other's back, so to speak, and so I did the same with you. I think these trees, separate root systems or one, work together as one tree."

"Should we look at ground level?" Anoo asks with a twinkle in his eye.

"Neighbors, lovers, brothers, I'm comfortable not knowing. Let's walk," says Laurel.

After slowly walking awhile Laurel points to a blossoming thistle with a bumblebee searching for nectar. As they watch, a sphinx moth goes to a flower right next to the bumblebee. The moth's wings don't seem to be touching the bumblebee, but the bee must feel the little breeze and the vibrations from the wings of the moth. The bumblebee leaves its flower and turns in a little circle until facing the moth. The bee's wings increase in pitch and the bee flies forward until it strikes the moth on its side. There is an audible little bonk as they collide. The moth then moves over to a nearby flower and continues feeding. The bee goes back to its flower and does the same.

"Well, that was interesting," says Anoo. "Did the bee smack the moth because it assessed the moth's proximity as a rudeness, as an intrusion?"

"That's what it looked like. But is that anthropomorphizing too much?"

"There are plenty of other thistle flowers around for the bee to choose to go to," notices Anoo.

"That's true for the moth also before there was ever conflict," says Laurel.

"Okay," agrees Anoo. "The moth ignored the bee and the bee responded by bonking the moth into awareness. The moth maybe said to itself 'no big deal' and went over to another flower. The bee went back to its original flower even though, without the intrusion, it probably would have already moved off to another flower."

"With the possibility of mutual anthropomorphizing that's how I interpret what we saw also. I wouldn't say the bee considered the moth's action as rude but as a physical intrusion. And the moth didn't have a clear thought of 'no big deal'; it just acted like it did. I give the nod of awareness and action to the bee and only patterned behavior to the moth. And yet the moth may have been aware of the bee all along and expected it to move off based on other encounters in the past."

"And the bee was hungrier or feistier than the moth expected," finishes Anoo.

"Which way would you go then?" asks Laurel. "The bee clearly set its action up. Did the moth only react to the bee's action or was it aware of the bee all along and didn't expect the bee to act the way it did based on the memory of past encounters?"

"I'll go with 'I don't know' as my conclusion. I'd have to watch other encounters before deciding."

"I'll agree with that conclusion, knowing my own comfort with delaying specific conclusions to gain information through communication and learning," states Laurel. "And hopefully adding accuracy to the conclusion."

"Conclusions that are not supported by a credible level of information are a hindrance to future learning," says Anoo.

"Conclusions that are based on feelings are often conclusions that are too vague to teach to others without resorting to 'don't think—obey' by the so-called teacher," adds Laurel, remembering their past conversation.

"Conclusions based on feelings are often egotistically based because the product of the conclusion is a feeling, not a valid explanation of the conclusion," continues Anoo.

"The validity of feelings-based conclusions is often skewed by the individual doing a better job of remembering when they are right than when they are wrong. Which is a very human thing to do. That's why that potential error should be constantly considered and certainly not ignored. Denial or a lack of awareness does not create accuracy in perspective," states Laurel.

"And the perception of the accuracy of conclusions based on

feelings is often skewed by misinterpretation."

"What misinterpretation?" prompts Laurel.

"The amount of time it takes to reach a feelings-based conclusion decreases over time. As a person becomes more familiar with the process, the process speeds up."

"Which to some can be misinterpreted as an increase in accuracy," concludes Laurel. "I think we hold a lot of similar value systems. Why do you think that is? Similar personalities or similar teachers using similar examples? Maybe we both, independently, stumbled on the most efficient way for humans to learn and grow?"

"I'll definitely lean away from the last and towards the first two. But I don't know which contributes the most."

"Then let's walk," states Laurel.

She turns and starts walking and Anoo takes a step to follow when Laurel stops and turns and looks at him. Anoo steps forward.

"What is it, Laurel?"

"Similar teachers. We were set up! Your great-uncle and my grandfather know each other."

"We haven't bumped into each other out here before but they certainly would have," agrees Anoo.

"They certainly would have," repeats Laurel. "And they would have recognized each other as kindred spirits. I think we should go back and kick their asses."

Anoo looks Laurel in the eye and says, "I, for one, Laurel, am going to thank my uncle for giving us the opportunity to meet."

"If your uncle is as good a man as my grandfather then I must admit it's reassuring to know they wanted us to meet."

"I'm sure they are both good men. With no malice of any kind towards either of us. They would only wish us the best."

Considering that, Laurel looks Anoo in the eye, her heart warms, her body relaxes, and she smiles and tilts her head a little to one side. As a dreamy look comes upon her face she closes her eyes while slowly sliding her hands up to her elbows and hugs herself. As she turns and walks away Anoo thinks, *Oh, what a good day this is.*

After following Laurel for a half mile or so through the aspens Anoo sees a downed log just ahead. Laurel walks up to it, sits down on the ground, and leans back. Anoo sits a couple of feet away and takes some water out of his pack. He offers it to Laurel and then drinks some too.

"Tell me more about your winter place, Laurel. How did you come to be there? What's the general layout?"

"It used to be a large ranch. A main house, some quarters for ranch hands, various barns, sheds, and corrals. That sort of thing. When my grandfather first came across the place it was deserted."

"When was that?"

"About forty years ago. He started fixing the place up by repairing and cleaning one of the smaller cabins. That became his base camp when he was away from town. When Grandfather was there he continued to work on the place. He fixed up a couple sheds and corrals, got a small irrigation ditch working, and then started bringing other people out to help."

"Your grandmother?"

"I think she went sometimes. They weren't committed to each other at that time. It was mostly friends from town at first. Together they got a lot done. They basically took the main house apart and used it for construction material. Now there's a half-dozen cabins, even more sheds, and several barns. About two dozen people stay there depending on the season. There isn't a fixed number of people. Sometimes people live in town for a while. There's usually some movement between there and town except in the middle of winter. Our main trips being spring and fall as I was saying yesterday. There really can't be more people without having less animals or the water would run out."

"Do you have any wells?"

"One, that we use for drinking water. It doesn't have a high rate of flow but runs steady all year. They've tried to dig a couple others but didn't reach water. The stream runs best in spring of course. It's usually dry by mid-summer. All the rain water off the roofs is saved. There's stock tanks and cisterns that we fill every spring. It's enough but we certainly can't be extravagant with water."

"Are all the people related now?"

"Some are but more are friends and neighbors from town. There's been a couple wanderers that have stuck around too. You'd be interested in the plum patch."

"We have a few berry patches and a small orchard. What's your plum patch?"

"There's a flat area next to the stream that bumps up against a short, steep north-facing hill. On the flat area, there was a patch of plums that were just little shrubs when my grandfather first started going there. After the carpentry, garden, and pasture work was well on its way he started working on the plums. He thinned out the oldest and most deformed of the small shrub-sized trees and started tending what was left. Now it's a couple acres of ten- to fifteen-foot-tall trees that I can walk between. Every fall we harvest the plums and make sauces, jams, and pies."

"How do you harvest the plums? Do you climb the trees?"

"They're way too thorny for that. We spread blankets under a tree and then we shake the plums free, gather them up, and move to another."

"That sounds efficient. What sort of yield do you have?"

"It is very efficient when the plums are ripe enough. We also keep the goats under there. They keep the vegetation under the trees in control and it gives them shade in the summer. Farming has its good and bad years as you obviously know. I'd say an average yield is well over a thousand pounds a year."

"What do you do for fuel?"

"There's the cottonwoods and some boxelder. The plums always need pruning too. Mostly though, every week we're up here someone takes a horse and a travois full of lodgepole back to winter camp. Not the big fat ones. The nice lodgepole size that they're named after. That size is good for building and fire."

"That sounds like a lot of work."

"A horse can pull quite a bit loaded that way. Walking speed they cover about fifteen miles a day, so four days to get there. After a day's rest, it only takes two days to ride back. About a week round trip and then someone else is ready to go when they get back. Tell me more about your place, Anoo."

"I wasn't around yet when my parents moved there, well, *back* there for my father. He lived there when it was his father's farm before his father, my grandfather, died from a farming accident. My parents had been living in my mother's family home in town. Then my parents, uncle, and my aunt fixed up the house and barn. There's some coops and sheds now too."

"Your aunt?" asks Laurel.

"Cassie, she's my mother's sister. She lives in their family's house now. Since then we've developed garden soils, grown orchard trees—the place is very efficient now."

"Your parents' names?"

"Eli and Tohlee."

"Your uncle?"

"Mateen. Your grandfather?"

"I just call him Grandfather. I don't know his first name. I think there's a history there he wants to keep to himself. I don't care. I love him," Laurel explains. "If you start your own farm it would be a lot of work to get to the efficiency of your parents' farm."

"That it would. It would basically be a decades-long project."

"I think it could lead to a very rewarding life," says Laurel.

Anoo looks at Laurel. She's looking straight ahead. He looks at her many long, tight braids. Each one is tied with a little thong of leather decorated with a couple of beads. He shifts his glance to her face. Dark complexion with full lips. She's still looking ahead but he knows that she is aware of him looking. Under her shawl she's wearing a sleeveless blouse. He glances at her chest and sees a small swell of breast. Her legs are long and covered completely by her skirt. She's almost as tall as he is. Her moccasins go above her ankles and up under her skirt. Very much an attractive woman. Then she turns toward him and says, "Now it's my turn." Anoo looks at her and smiles. Then he looks ahead. She likes his profile. His beard is trimmed close. His hair isn't as long as hers but long. It's pulled back tightly but as soon as it goes past his leather tie it curls out in several directions. She thinks it would be wavy if loose. His hands are heavy and strong-looking. Broad shoulders and strong thighs also. Very much an attractive man. She looks away. He looks back at her.

"You're an attractive woman, Laurel."

"Thank you. I'm glad you think so. And you're an attractive man, Anoo."

"Thank you right back. I like getting to know you, our conversations, and being together."

"I feel the same, Anoo. Just how much time can we have together?"

"I was going to go back to Mateen's tonight and then home tomorrow."

"Is that still what you want to do?" she asks a little nervously. "To go back home tomorrow? I'd like to spend more time with you."

"That's what I was thinking before we met. Now, I'll still go back to Mateen's tonight but I think I can stay a few more days. I very much want to spend more time with you. Fall harvest will be starting soon though. There's plenty of preparation work to do before then."

"Like what?"

"Root cellars to clean out, tools to sharpen, pots and drying racks to prepare. That sort of thing."

"Are your parents expecting you tomorrow?"

"Yes, but Mateen can tell my father what I'm doing."

"Carrier pigeon?"

"Well, carrier thoughts," Anoo says with a smile.

"That sounds like our next conversation," says Laurel. "Is that a connection you're working on? You said you were working on connections when we talked about your perceiving out on a string. Connections like my sensing you just before we first met and

54

perceiving away from the body in a dream state."

"Yes, those and carrier pigeon thought connections. I'm still work-ing on the connection part. You can help me with that another time. Let's talk about the carrier pigeon part itself."

"Okay, but can we count on three more days together?"

"I think so. I can tell you for sure tomorrow. I'm sure another day is fine and three should be. A couple more days after that is even a possibility. But that's pushing things. They're counting on me."

"I'm glad they count on you and I hope they can spare you. Should we meet out here mid-morning and be together until late afternoon? I want to make sure when we part we know how we see ourselves. As two people learning about each other so they're closer in the future or as two people that happened to bump into each other and go their separate ways."

"I want to know also and I'm very much leaning towards being closer in the future. We can certainly go to Mateen's if it turns stormy over the next few days. But I like being out here with you."

"I very much like the sound of that. Let's eat and talk about carrier pigeon thoughts."

As they eat they become absorbed in their surroundings instead of talking. They're in an aspen stand with heavy undergrowth and trees that are well spaced and fifty to sixty feet tall. The aspens' leaves are all above forty feet up. The light green trunks with black accents spread out under the rustling green canopy like pillars holding up a roof. Birds are flying and calling and insects are chirping. There are a few biting flies but not enough to make them move. Shafts of sunlight are coming down to the ground between the canopies of the trees. As a breeze stirs the high-up leaves the shafts of light waver and blur at the edges. They watch as a small cloud passes in front of the sun, causing shafts to go out and turn back on as the shadow from the cloud moves across the stand. They watch a doe walking through the trees. She seems to be more bothered by the flies than they are as she shakes her head periodically and is moving like she has someplace to go. An errant breeze comes below the canopy and moves through the undergrowth. It brushes against them and blows on by. Laurel half turns toward Anoo.

"This is beautiful!" she says. "What a spectacular setting to share with you and to get to know you in. Carrier thoughts are telepathy of course."

"They are. Telepathy I'll define as nonverbal communication with words in English."

"As compared to empathy, which is nonverbal communication of feelings or impressions. Keep going."

"I think they are very similar forms of communication. I would say telepathy is an extension of empathy that is the result of an individual developing clarity of mind by choosing their own value systems."

"That would mean empathy is more generalized and telepathy is a more specific communication through a similar connection," Laurel concludes.

"Yes, anything that can be verbally communicated in English can be communicated telepathically."

"So, if one is communicating a feeling as compared to the word describing that same feeling empathy would be the more accurate form of communication."

"I guess that's right, Laurel. The words representing feelings do not contain the feeling themselves. Which is where the inherent error in logic comes in. Sentences that are very factual are easier to interpret through logic than sentences containing words that represent emotions."

"Because words representing emotions are just that, a representation, as compared to a definition perhaps, or an example. I think I understand that aside topic and we could keep going along that path but let's stick with telepathy."

"Okay, I should then say empathy and telepathy are similar forms of communication each with their own pluses and minuses."

"I like that better. Keep going."

"I'll use Mateen and my father as an example. When I go back to the cabin this afternoon I'll tell Mateen I want to stay at least three more days. That won't be a problem with him. It does need to be communicated to my parents so they don't think I'm out here with a broken leg and Mateen needs help finding me or caring for me. Going from his description to me of the process Mateen will imagine or visualize my father as though he is standing right in front of him. The feeling of friendship with my father and past shared experiences aid that visualization. Then he will focus on communication with my father. A level of communication that requires concentration like explaining a difficult, detailed concept. Not a 'hey, how are you' conversation."

"Detailed like this conversation. Which is where the clarity you mentioned earlier comes in. Go ahead."

"That concentration by Mateen will then be picked up by my father because of the past connections between them."

"Past connections meaning telepathic connections?"

"At this point with the two of them, yes, because of a history of such connections. But it can start just with the familiarity people reach with others by sharing experiences."

"Like how empathetic connections can start. Okay."

"Mateen won't want to intrude, so he will basically ask my father if he is available to communicate."

"How would he be intruding?"

"Well…" says Anoo, turning and looking at Laurel questioningly.

She says, "There is no topic of conversation I wouldn't want to discuss with you. This is just the conversation we're having right now."

"Okay. When I first got to Mateen's cabin a couple days ago we wanted to let my parents know I'd arrived safely. Mateen connected with my father and then basically excused himself from the conversation. My parents were up at their swimming hole."

"What's the problem there? Were they skinny-dipping and Mateen could see them?"

"I don't think there is that kind of visual detail in telepathic communications."

"Maybe so and maybe not. Let's not limit ourselves or telepathy itself."

"I do like you, Laurel. They probably were naked as they usually do skinny-dip. They also like to indulge their physical desires for each other there."

"There? Outside in broad daylight?" she says, feigning astonishment.

"Yes." Anoo smiles. "It's private. I don't think they've ever been disturbed by anyone unexpected."

"Ever?"

"As far as I know and that means many hundreds of times over the years."

"What a nice way to spend an afternoon. Did Mateen then let them know you had arrived safely or would that have constituted an intrusion?"

"I think that would have been an intrusion, so I don't think he did specifically. My father would have expected contact and known everything was okay though. If there had been an emergency Mateen would have intruded."

"In this case the communication was without specific words. The communication would have ended up, to avoid an intrusion, more on the empathetic level," states Laurel.

"You're right about that. That shows the similarities in the two types of communication."

"And that telepathy involves more focus and specific communication than empathy. As Mateen pulled back from a telepathic connection to an empathetic one to avoid intrusion while still communicating the essential information," Laurel concludes and after thinking for a second, "You said *their* swimming hole?"

"I did. I have my own downstream closer to the farm."

They sit for a few minutes without talking. Each is considering what sort of person the other must be for this and earlier conversations to flow the way they have. Conversations that have very quickly gone beyond the norm. They look out at the aspen grove. The shafts of light are angled more but still distinct. The birds and insects haven't been paying attention to their conversation. The aspen stand is pretty much the same. There is a change. The connection between them is growing.

"I'm sure we can continue on the subject of telepathy but let's walk," says Laurel.

Anoo stands and reaches out his hand to her. She accepts his offer. Standing up and leaning in almost close enough to him to kiss, she looks him in the eye and says thank you. Then turns and walks away. Anoo follows her as she wanders through the stand and then to the edge where they can look far to the east. Between two hills they can see several lower hills reaching down to the plains, which stretch out to the horizon. Laurel reaches into her carry bag, which has one strap over her shoulder and her shawl. She takes out the small bone flute she brought.

"I wanted to bring you a gift also. I thought you might enjoy playing this when you're out in the woods alone. Have you ever played one?"

"I haven't."

"It's surprising how much capability for music such a small simple instrument can have."

"I thank you, Laurel. It is a thoughtful gift. I actually brought two gifts for you."

Taking his pack off Anoo finds the packet of spices he brought from the cabin.

"I'm sure you have your own spices. But I thought maybe some of these would be new or not commonly available to you. I hope you and your people will enjoy them. My mother put them together for Mateen. She usually sends more than he can use."

"I thank you for your gift, Anoo. It also is a thoughtful gift. I'm sure we will appreciate it."

With that they find a place to sit and enjoy the view. Anoo explores his new flute while Laurel smells the variety of spices in the packet. After being together for a while, Laurel stands up and puts her bag back over her shoulder. Anoo puts his flute away, stands, and moves his pack into a comfortable position. Laurel turns and goes uphill to the top of the ridge and her trail back to camp.

"I guess I'm ready to go back to camp, Anoo. I do want to say that if we weren't meeting again tomorrow I'd wring every minute out of our day together I could."

"And I, Laurel, would follow you back to camp even if you were throwing sticks and stones at me."

"But they break bones."

"I think I would prefer that kind of pain over not seeing you again."

"A little much, but I like the sentiment. I'd like to hug you good-bye, Anoo. May I?"

"Please, allow me Miss Laurel, it would be my honor and privilege."

They step up to each other. Looking Laurel in the eye Anoo reaches his hands out and runs them slowly from her forearms to her shoulders. Laurel returns Anoo's look and very deliberately raises her hands and places them on his hips. Anoo leans forward, slides his hands around her shoulders and pulls her close. As he does Laurel slides her hands up and around his waist. As their bodies touch they both slightly adjust their positions and then they fully embrace. Laurel feels her body relax and she melts into Anoo. Anoo feels his spine stiffen and straighten. It feels like his arms have grown longer with the need to wrap around her. He smells rose in her hair. Laurel smells man at his neck. They hold each other. Then Anoo rubs his hands around and over her shoulder blades and hugs her close again. Laurel moves her hands up to the middle of his back and squeezes him firmly against her chest. Then she puts her hands back on his hips and lightly pushes away. Anoo leans back and puts his hands on her shoulders. He runs his hands slowly down her arms to her wrists as she lets go of his hips and then he runs his fingertips along the backs of her hands. He stops and turns his hands palms up. Laurel slides her fingers toward him until their palms are touching. They take a step back as their hands go to their sides. She looks Anoo in the eyes and says with a smile on her face, "Now I'm going to go back to camp and kick my grandfather's ass."

Anoo laughs and responds, "Don't be too hard on him. I want to meet your grandfather and thank him."

"I'll see. Anoo, thank you for a better than imaginable hug, conversations, and day together."

"It was every bit as good a day for me, Laurel. I can't imagine a better way to start our day together tomorrow than to hug you again."

Laurel turns and looking back over her shoulder with a smile says, "Then go take a shower."

Back at camp Laurel goes and finds her grandfather.

"You dawg. You ole dawg."

"I can't imagine what you're referring to, my beautiful blossoming, multi-petaled flower. The depth of your multifaceted personality reflected by your namesake leaves me only able to wonder at what you could be referring to."

"Nice try, you old dawg. How long have you known Mateen?"

"Almost as long as I've been going to winter camp. After enough work had been done at our winter home to be comfortable I was able to start exploring this far. I ran into him pretty early on after that."

"You recognized him as a kindred spirit?"

"That happened pretty much right away upon our meeting."

"Do you see each other very often?"

"I wouldn't say every year. But most summers we meet up for news and because we like each other's company."

"Has he been to winter camp?"

"A couple times many years ago. The last time you were two years old, I think. He met you but I wouldn't expect you'd remember."

"Have you been to his place?"

"A fair number of times. I've never met Anoo or his parents. Some of the times that I've left summer camp for a night or two I would go there."

"I told Anoo I was going to kick your ass."

"What did he say to that?"

"He said he wanted to thank you and Mateen."

"And you?"

"Grandfather," she says, while throwing her arms around him. "Thank you."

"How happy for you can I be?"

"This is so new and just plain so...new. I think we've had great conversations. I enjoy his perspective. I enjoy walking with him, sitting with him, being with him. I'm pleasantly surprised at just how much I like being with him. I told him if we weren't seeing each other tomorrow I'd have wrung every minute out of this day with him I could."

"And how do you think he feels about you?"

"I think the same. I don't think that's my own deep level of hoping so."

"Is he saying he enjoys being with you?"

"Yes."

"I'm sure he's a very straightforward young man and you can take him at his word. What will you do tomorrow?"

"We're going to meet around mid-morning. That's all we've talked about. More of the same. Seeing what it's like spending time together."

"You are the light of my life, Laurel. Nothing would please me more than seeing you happy with a good man. My best wishes to you."

"Thank you, Grandfather. Thank you! Thank you! Thank you! For everything over the years and now this."

"Hello, my young friend."

"Good afternoon to you, Mateen."

"What are you thinking? A drink? A shower? Dinner? Feeling manipulated?"

"A shower and then a drink and dinner. There really wasn't much of a feeling of being manipulated. What feelings of manipulation there were went far away a couple hours ago when I hugged Laurel good-bye for the day."

"For the day?"

"Yes, I told her I could probably stay for three more days and maybe a couple more if possible. First, is that okay with you?"

"Of course it is. You know that but I appreciate your asking."

"Can you let my parents know?"

"Sure. Three days and maybe more?"

"I'm sure three more will be fine. A couple more after that might be too little time to prepare for harvest."

"Okay, take a shower and I'll let you know."

After the shower Anoo is feeling relaxed and ready to talk some more.

"There's a drink for you. I'm sure that the shower was refreshing."

"I feel great. What did my father say?"

"He said he'll help you be definitive. Four more days with Laurel. The next to travel home. And after that you're back to work."

"Thank you for that."

"Tell me about Laurel."

"I'm not sure I could say anything that wasn't just a string of superlatives. I think she's a very attractive, intelligent, perceptive, thoughtful woman."

"Well, that certainly sounds like a good base to build a friendship on. I'll let you put things into perspective on your own. How about a little philosophizing?"

"Okay, but I'd like to know how you met…Grandfather? What do you call him?"

"My friend. I never bothered to push. How we met? I was up in these hills before he was. I didn't make it out as far as his place to the east until after we got to know each other. Shortly after he started exploring these hills I started noticing his tracks and then his campfire. Then we met. We got along right away and it turned into a very nice long friendship."

"That sounds like a fortuitous meeting. It resulted in a long friendship and contact that gives you information about things happening in a different place and connected to a different town. Philosophizing—what new thoughts and perspectives have you had?"

"Ah, my young friend, that question I'm going to turn back around to you."

"Okay, I've been thinking that evolution is more than a statement of the history of life on Earth."

"Meaning life on other planets, or as solar systems change over time the same as galaxies or individual stars change over time?"

"Well, yes, those too, but I was thinking of the base or perspective people perceive the world around them from."

"Okay, make your point," says Mateen.

"I'm thinking evolution puts people in a timeline of, hopefully, increasing knowledge and awareness. A timeline where people need to learn and change and grow. I think creationism creates a delusion of grandeur in people. The whole concept is about how people are the center of the universe and God's greatest creation. This creates a perspective that we are already at a peak of exceptionality because of what has been given to us, not what we have grown ourselves into. I think that perspective actually inhibits learning both individually and from a societal standpoint. I see evolution as open-ended change."

"I like that idea. The evolution of humans is a type of moral compass because of the understanding of where we are in the process. It's not just a history of life on Earth. Choosing to believe in evolution or in creationism is one of the choices in value systems one can intentionally make. Okay, give me something else."

"I was thinking I came up with a day-to-day example of how people create evil in their lives. Something other than the obvious examples of violence against one another."

"You're not going to bore me with some form of 'the devil made me do it,' are you?"

"I would be embarrassed if I did. I was thinking people create evil in their daily lives when a person looks out from themselves and sees someone more than what they are. A person more intelligent or better able to communicate or more capable in some way. Then they try to tear that more capable person down so that they can feel better about themselves."

"I like that. Evil then is the responsibility of the individual, not some deity. Both your examples amount to the idea that focus on superior or supreme beings can take away from individual responsibility or action. For example, Christians who use the idea that Jesus will physically be coming back to Earth to set things right as justification not to act themselves to make something better now. Interesting stuff, Anoo. Now I'd like to tell you again about the difference I see between Americans and citizens of this Country of Freedom."

"I'd like to hear that again. I'm thinking you're going back over the basics for me in my time of questioning where my life is going."

"You're a perceptive young man. The difference I'm talking about can be defined. First, from a technical standpoint the freedoms in this Country's Constitution are freedoms protecting individuals from governmental oppression. I think those same freedoms can be applied to an individual's actions without the government being involved. To me, an American is an individual that applies the concepts of freedom of speech, press, and religion in their daily lives as they interact with others. A citizen of this Country of Freedom merely happens to live here. They live here with intolerance of others. With intolerance of differences. They react to differences of appearance, language, religion, country of origin, gender, and sexuality with superiority, hatred, and violence. They actively divide humanity into categories.

Americans are individuals that intentionally unite humanity through compassionate tolerance no matter what country they live in. Being an American is an individual goal, not something given through birthplace or citizenship. Americans unite people through their respect for other's freedoms. They verbally reject authoritarianism and dictatorship. They are the voices in the crowd that sing out, 'The king has no clothes.'"

Chapter Four

ANOO WAKES BEFORE sunrise after a nice night's sleep. He showers and eats breakfast and has a little chat with Mateen. Then he heads back to his meeting place with Laurel. Along the way he takes his time, enjoying the walk. When he gets to the rocky hill where he has been watching the meteor shower he takes a long look around. Everything looks fine, so he keeps going. He drops down, crosses the narrow valley bottom and then climbs up to the top of the rocky ridge to the trail Laurel uses. Before long Laurel walks up and stands in front of him.

"Good morning to you, Laurel."

"And to you, Anoo."

"How's your grandfather?"

"I let him off easy; he'll be able to walk by the time we're ready to go back to winter camp," she says with a smile.

Anoo gives a little smiling laugh and holds out his hands.

"My turn this time to be the lead hugger," says Laurel.

She runs her hands up Anoo's arms and stops with her palms against the ends of his shoulders. She leans her head back and gives him an impressed little smile and he smiles back. She runs her hands over his shoulders and around his neck. Pulling him in and down a little she feels her body contact his. She feels his strong arms around her back as he pulls her closer. Her body relaxes and she feels his body from her cheek to her thighs. They both enjoy the contact for a while. She moves back and hold his hands in hers asking, "Did

Mateen carrier pigeon your father?"

"He did. My father said I can have four more days, then back to work. May I have the pleasure of your company for those days?"

"It would be my pleasure. And now what do you think? A walk? A talk?"

"Let's walk some while it's still a little cool. I think today is going to be a hot one. How about going west this morning?"

"Okay, you lead."

They walk slowly through the trees and meadows. Generally heading west but letting the contours of the land direct them also. The game trails they are walking on don't allow them to be side by side. They walk just fast enough to see new things, a little faster than a stalk. They stop in the trees just before the edges of clearings, looking to see what is there. Not out of fear of predators but because of their own curiosity. If they see something interesting they watch, if not, they slowly move on. At one point Anoo gestures ahead and a little left. Laurel isn't sure what he sees as they move in that direction. Then she sees the tops of pine trees sticking well above a clump of aspen. As they walk under the ponderosas they are a little in awe of their solidness and obvious age. The trees are thick-limbed and -trunked and relatively close together. They find a spot where a downed trunk crosses a patch of needles and sit down. They drink some water and look at each other.

"Talking time?" asks Laurel.

Anoo nods and says, "What sort of topic?"

"How about interesting subjects but cover some ground too."

"Okay, but I'm not sure what you mean. You start."

"I could start talking about a supreme being but you did say the universe has had thousands and thousands of intelligent species and trillions and trillions of intelligent individuals come and go. Because a supreme being is aware of every leaf that falls it has all the experiences of those beings included in its awareness."

"And I would probably add some zeros to those numbers. Both for the individuals and the species. I absolutely think evolution is a more accurate statement of the history of life on Earth than creationism. It is a more exact and clear statement. I think there is some mythical truth to creationism. I'm not buying the timeline by any means, but there could have been flooding that severely impacted humanity for example. I just wouldn't attribute that to a vengeful god that wanted to direct humanity's evolution toward a selected set of people. 'Vengeance is mine sayeth the lord,' but I see vengeance as a human trait. Not the trait of a being that has incorporated the experiences of trillions upon trillions of individual lives from a myriad of species into its perspective."

"Does your version of a superior being use punishment?" asks Laurel.

"I have no need for a vengeful or punishing god. I create my own religion and am not concerned with being punished for that. I'll accept my own mistakes and try to learn from them. I prefer that to accepting an existing perspective and its inevitable mistakes."

"How about natural disasters?"

"Just that—natural. Not the result of a vengeful god's punishment."

"How about evil?"

"The product of ugly people's behavior."

"And the idea that the greatest trick the devil has ever played on people is to convince them that he doesn't exist?" queries Laurel.

"I prefer the concept that the greatest trick the devil ever played was to convince people that he exists. People learn more when evil is the product of their own actions and so their own individual responsibility. Evil as the product of a deity's actions or trickery contributes too much to individuals being able to avoid responsibility for their actions."

"A trait that is much too common in people," Laurel comments. "What if that deity actually exists?"

"I'll have to see him first."

"How about good?" continues Laurel.

"'Do unto others' stretches back at least to Confucius. Jesus of Nazareth taught to aid the sick and poor and less fortunate."

"And Confucius may have been taught by an elder," posits Laurel. "How about evil is necessary to appreciate good."

"The most credit I'd give that idea is that one murder should be enough to teach a billion people for their entire lifetimes that murder is wrong."

"Back to evolution. Does a universal god influence human evolution?"

"I prefer the idea that humans have been given dominion over life on Earth by that god. Life on Earth includes humans. I think dominion over ourselves gives us responsibility for our own evolution."

"Alien species that haven't lived their history to extinction yet have influenced life on Earth?"

"I've never seen the idea disproved and there's no good reason to consider it impossible."

"Those alien species have existed and will again but just won't overlap humanity's time on Earth," Laurel states but is also asking.

"Galaxies usually contain many similarly aged stars. I think there is enough time and numbers of solar systems involved for some overlap. I wouldn't discredit alien intervention in human evolution because of the impossibility of an overlap."

"Does a universal god influence individual humans?"

"I prefer to think our fate is what we make. Thus increasing our individual and societal responsibility and freedom. If that god has to save us from ourselves it would be because of our own error in directing ourselves."

"We were made in God's image. Does that mean God has two legs and arms and breathes air?" asks Laurel.

"I prefer to think that God's image of itself is that of a self-determined being. We were made by God to be self-determined. Creators of our own future. As a species and as individuals."

"Let's move on. Beauty is in the eye of the beholder?" suggests Laurel.

"Absolutely and that goes for truth also."

"A little more depth please."

"A firm believer raised in, and surrounded by, one organized religion feels as much truth in that religion as an individual raised in and surrounded by a different organized religion. To put it another way—the parental love for a child, or love between a couple, is just as strong in people of other religions, races, or societies."

"Truth or beauty then is a statement of familiarity, not an established universal base that is reached," Laurel restates. "That fits with your independent perspective idea we talked about yesterday. The base of individual truth or beauty given by a society or religion one grows up with can be changed by individual choice and intent. That choice creates the individual's own value system, base in other words, that they perceive their own independent perspective from."

"Very well put. And during that development of the value systems that make up an individual's base there is doubt and confusion and mistakes and, compared to those that adopt an existing system, there is a lack of developmental speed, at least at first. In the long run the lack is with the adopters of existing structures."

"That was a fun little speed round of concepts. I'm going to take a quick break," says Laurel.

She wanders away. Making sure Anoo is out of sight she removes the cloth she wears around her chest to hold her breasts in and puts it and her shawl in her carry bag. She adjusts her clothes, takes a deep breath, and goes back to Anoo.

"Well, hello, Laurel, it's nice to see you."

"You were just seeing me."

"I'm seeing more of you now than I was."

"Yeah, well, this is me more relaxed. Like at night when I'm sitting around a fire in camp. I want to be relaxed with you."

"You're bigger than you show when you wear your chest cloth."

"I don't find it comfortable to be flopping around as I work. It feels good to be walking in the woods like this though. Anoo, I want to know where you think this is heading? Us, that is. When it comes right down to it if this was a fling on a solstice we'd have been rolling around naked the first night. What do you think this is?"

"I'm thinking my timing is bad. We should have met on a solstice."

"That would mean this is a fling."

"I was absolutely joking, Laurel. I cannot believe how much of a connection I feel with you and how fast it's happened. I think you are an incredibly attractive, intelligent, thoughtful, perceptive woman. To me, this is not about a passionate fling with you. I'm leaning towards a thousand joinings with you."

"A thousand? So not a fling, but you're going to leave me after one single year? That's the best you have to offer?"

"Ha ha, oh, Laurel. I like you so much. Okay, thousands and thousands and thousands of joinings. I think this is about us coming together as a couple. And what are you thinking?"

"I so like the sound of that, Anoo. And who am I to argue with your description of me?" Laurel adds, laughing, "Okay, I want this to be about us coming together as a couple too. A long-term couple. I'm thinking I'm going to want us to have to spoon when we join because of my big, fat, swollen, pregnant belly. I'm thinking we'll be joining and interrupted by the cry of our child. I'm hoping we'll want to run to the nearest haystack as soon as our kids leave for school because I'll want you to give me a thumping. I'll want you to be inside me for hours at a time. I'm thinking I want your life to revolve around me as mine will around you."

"As fast as this is, I think I'm falling in love with you, Laurel."

"As fast as this is, that's what I'm thinking too, Anoo. Let's go for a walk and let this sink in."

With that Laurel stands directly in front of Anoo. She bends her knees down and holds out her hands. He reaches up and takes hers. She has to do most of the lifting at first because of the way he is leaning against the downed tree trunk. Anoo feels the strength in her arms as she pulls and then the strength in her legs as she lifts. He feels his weight go down to his feet and steadies himself. Laurel moves their hands down to their sides and leans in until her breasts touch his chest. Then she leans in further and kisses his cheek. Anoo lets go of her hands to hold her and she turns and steps away. Laughing she calls over her shoulder, "Let's run!"

She runs ahead of him and they quickly leave the large ponderosas behind. They cross a small meadow and go through an aspen stand. Then, they're out the other side and through another meadow into a larger aspen stand. In the middle of that stand the trees thin and they're into a patch of hellebore. Laurel holds her arms out away from her sides and runs with her hands touching the tasseled tops like she's flying. Then she pretends she is diving off the trail and disappears under the plants in a crouch. The hellebore is so tall all Anoo can see are the tops of the plants moving where she is. He hears the squeaks of their leaves as she brushes plants against each other. Then she's back out on the trail and running in front of him again. She sees a spot ahead where tall larkspur is growing on either side of the trail. Dipping down a little and slowing she watches the flowers go by her face. Then she speeds up again until reaching the edge of the grove. She stops with her heart and lungs pumping. Anoo catches up and stops with his hands on her shoulders. After catching his breath, he slowly reaches up to her neck. Wrapping his hands around her many braids he holds her hair up and away from the back of her neck. "That was fun!" she says as she fans her hand at her bare neck and with a "Thank you!" to Anoo she starts walking.

They go through a large meadow with rocks scattered throughout. The next aspen stand is small but under the tallest and thickest trees is a patch of ferns. Laurel motions Anoo to stop and walks ahead a bit. Going off the trail she turns a quick circle back toward Anoo. She stops behind a good-sized aspen and gets down on her hands and knees. Then she pokes her head out from behind the trunk and under a fern. Fronds frame her face like a decorative hat. They laugh and she comes back out on the trail. Anoo motions for her to wait. He goes back up the trail fifty feet to an aspen branch with a dozen yellow leaves on it. It was probably an elk walking down the trail that broke the branch and left it dangling, coloring the leaves because of stress, not season. He breaks the branch off and goes back to Laurel. Standing in front of her he breaks off a yellow leaf and works it into a braid. One by one he adds more, up the left side of her face and down the right. Stepping away he motions her back to the fern. She goes back behind the aspen and pokes her head out from under the fern again. She moves the green fronds until they frame her dark brown face. The yellow leaves run down her black hair like drops of sunshine. Anoo thinks he's never seen anyone so beautiful. He stands and looks until Laurel comes back out on the trail. She looks at him and he says, "You're the most beautiful woman I've ever seen!" Laurel smiles, turns, and skips down the trail. With her heart full from Anoo's compliment and her back to him she raises her arms above her head and yells, "Woohoo!" and she runs.

She crosses a little meadow and stops just inside some more aspens. Peering out from around a trunk she watches Anoo come out into the meadow. He's already slowed and looked around a second before coming out in the open and now looks all around the meadow. Thinking she didn't go far he walks across the meadow. She thinks he looks like a man who is comfortable. He knows meadows and aspen. He looks like he's "here now." Not the "here now" of meditation, but of quiet awareness. The "being here now" where here is familiar from learning and experience. And the now is comfortable through competence. He seems to look right at her. He can't see her yet, but their eyes lock like animals who've just become aware of each other. They feel each other drawn together. It's like they are standing next to each other looking deep in each other's eyes. Laurel thinks of after their first meeting when their eyes locked across the rocky valley. He walks up to her and she closes her eyes. He sees she has her arms and one leg wrapped around an aspen in a tight hug. He walks up and she opens her eyes. Feigning surprise she says, "Oh, Anoo, how funny, I was just thinking of you."

She laughs and runs out of the trees and into a large rocky meadow. It starts to drop off steeply in front of her and she waits for Anoo.

"I know where we are," says Anoo. "Let's go down the hill to a place I know and get out of the sun."

"Okay. You know where we are? Are we near Mateen's cabin?"

"We're a few miles away. Below us is the stream that runs in front of his cabin. I've walked up to the headwaters before. That should be just below us."

They walk down a little and then drop down steeply into a narrow ravine where they can hear tumbling water. They get to the stream and climb up the bed a short way. The narrow ravine gets even steeper and becomes a series of little waterfalls. Most are just a couple of feet high but one is big enough to stand under. There are little ferns poking out of the thick green moss which covers the rocks near the spray of the falls.

"This is so beautiful, and cooler," says Laurel.

"I come up here sometimes to hang out and stand under the waterfall."

"So, you brought me here to bathe under the waterfall with you?"

"We could. If you'd like we can take turns."

"Hmmm, I'm hot and sticky. Let's get naked!"

With that Laurel strips so fast Anoo just watches. She stands in front of him naked. He slowly looks her up and down. Before he can get his thoughts together to compliment her she holds her hands up and gives him a "what about you" look. He strips too but is more awkward. She looks at his naked body and then walks up to him. Turning him around she pushes him under the waterfall. They take turns enjoying the delicious coolness on their naked bodies until they are a little chilled. Moving away from the water they walk out into full sun. As they dry in the bright August sunshine they quickly warm up. With the chill of the cool water gone they sit and enjoy the sun on their naked bodies.

"What should we do now, Anoo?"

Taking a long look at Laurel's arousing nakedness he says, "I guess we should start walking back. It'll be a little warm going back up the slope we came down. If we wait until the sun drops low enough for things to cool down though we won't be getting back before dark."

"That would cause my grandfather to worry."

"We don't want that and we can walk quickly through the sunny spots and linger in the shade as we go."

They keep a good pace up through the open meadows and stop in the shade for short breaks. During one break, they're standing in the shade when they see branches and vegetation sway and move in front of them. They watch the movements get closer and then a cool breeze washes over them. Anoo reaches his hands up to Laurel's shoulders, gently pulls her toward him, and kisses her hair. She looks back at him and smiles. Walking again it takes them a couple of hours to get back to the rocky ridge where they first met two days before. Facing each other Laurel takes Anoo's hands in hers.

"We have three more days together, Anoo."

"I've enjoyed our unexpected meeting and every moment with you since, Laurel. I look forward to seeing you again here, tomorrow morning."

"And I've been looking forward to this, Anoo."

Looking in his eyes Laurel lets go of Anoo's hands and reaches hers up to his shoulders and then around his neck. Anoo wraps his around her waist. They kiss. Pulling back a little to where their lips are just brushing against each other they move slightly and kiss again. A long, full kiss. Laurel takes her hands from around Anoo's neck and turns in his arms. She holds his hands to her stomach and leans back against him.

"I'm starting to feel like a couple with you, Anoo."

"I'm feeling like I want to be holding you like this when your hair has all turned gray."

"I like the way you feel about our future, the way your arms feel around me, your body against mine. Thank you for a wonderful, beautiful day. I'll see you in the morning."

Anoo watches as Laurel walks away. Almost out of sight she turns, they lock eyes, and she crosses her forearms in front of her in an X and hugs them to her.

"Well, hello there, my young friend. I'm sure you want to clean up, but relax and sit for a bit. Did you have a good day with Laurel?"

"It was a wonderful and special day. I'd like to have more days just like today with her."

"I'm glad for you. What are you thinking for your next three days?"

"More of the same, spending time together in a beautiful place as we get to know each other."

"I'm going to ask you a question that is more fitting of Laurel's grandfather. What are your intentions with her?"

"I am a little surprised you're asking."

"Then I'll explain. First, I want to know what you two are saying your intentions are."

"To spend the next few days getting to know each other. We haven't really talked about after that."

"Your intentions are already a factor. I would think you've talked some about this already. Intentions as to how you two are going to interact for these remaining days. I'm not referring to after that."

"Okay. I see. We're interacting to find out if we could be a couple. We're not looking at this as a chance meeting that will only result in a short fling."

"I think that's a good choice with her. I bring this up because I want you to consider the next few days. If this was going to be a fling with her and you join some over the next few days you could probably walk away and that would be that, at least until next year. If you join with her while exploring the option of being a couple with a newfound love for each other and everything works out well, I'm not so sure you'd be willing to spend the winter apart."

"I see what you mean. I haven't been thinking past the next few days. And yet we're pointing ourselves past that already."

"I'm certainly not bringing this up as a decision that needs to be made immediately. I just want you to be aware of the very big decision you may be setting yourselves up for in the very near future."

"If we fall in love and want to be a couple," finishes Anoo. "I guess there's only three likely options. Me with her at winter camp. Her with me at the farm. Or, we wait until spring to grow closer together. And your concerns with the third option are very realistic."

"Why don't you take a shower and think some."

After Anoo's shower and drinks in hand on the front porch Mateen starts the conversation again.

"Let's consider your first two options. The third can wait as long as you don't go off half-cocked looking for her in the middle of the winter."

"Okay, winter camp would be entirely new to me. The farm would be what I'm expecting to do at this point."

"Another winter at the farm would have an element of new to it if Laurel was there with you. To verify, the farm is what you've been thinking for this winter before you met Laurel?"

"I've been thinking I want to do something different. But I haven't been thinking of doing anything different this coming winter. If we're at the farm we would certainly impact my parents. I guess that's true for winter camp also."

"The impact at winter camp would probably be less because of the greater number of people involved. For your parents, I'm sure they would both want what is best for you. Sure, there would be some impact. I think the impact would be minimal. And as for your mother, I can picture her dancing in a circle while singing out, 'I'm going to have a daughter.' So, I don't see a real concern there. Also, I mentioned you might find it hard to be apart for the winter after falling in love. There is the idea of too much too soon to consider. Enjoy the view while I get dinner together."

"Hello, Grandfather."

"Hello, Laurel. Did you have a good day?"

"Better than I could have imagined. Did anything happen around here?"

"Nothing out of the ordinary. What will you be doing tomorrow?"

"Oh yeah, Anoo can stay up here for four more days. Today was one so three to go. Then he has to go back to work at the farm."

"Three more days together. Where do you think that will take you?"

"I guess I've only been thinking I want more of the same."

"Which is?"

"More growing together as a couple."

"So, three more days of growing together as a couple, successfully, I hope. And then?"

"And then? Well, I think I need dinner and a good long stare into a fire."

Laurel goes to the cooking fire and gets a bowl of soup and some corn tortillas for dinner. After helping clean up camp for the night, she gets her backrest and sits next to a watch fire. Her two favorite girlfriends bring their rests and set up next to her. While cleaning up camp she's already told them the highlights of her day. Not talking, all three sit with their shoulders touching. They watch the fire rise with new wood and die back down a couple of times. Then the friend on her right takes Laurel's hand in both of hers and lays her cheek on Laurel's shoulder. She says, "If you and your new man want to share each other's hearts and spirits like you share your body on a solstice and you're meant to be together, your spirits will merge and flow together like the waters of life on a solstice night. You're a good person, Laurel. Look into your heart and you'll know what to do." She kisses Laurel on the cheek and goes to bed. Laurel pushes her shoulder against her other friend, who puts her arm around her and pulls her head and brimming eyes down onto her lap. Stroking Laurel's hair she watches the constellations move across the sky as Laurel dreams dreams of love and comfort.

At the farm at the same time Laurel and Anoo are parting for the day Tohlee walks up to Eli.

"Eli, I can't contain myself. I have to tell Cassie that Anoo has met someone."

"I'm surprised you haven't already."

"I told her I wanted to see her tonight because of news from Anoo. She said to come over for dinner and to spend the night. Jed will be there, so you can talk to him while we girl talk."

"There really isn't that much to tell yet."

"He went to go watch the meteor shower and now wants a few more days because he met someone out in the woods. That's huge! We can talk about that for hours."

"Okay, I should have realized. Are we cleaning up, taking care of the animals, and going?"

"Yes please."

After walking to town and greeting Cassie and Jed the men and women go off to talk. Cassie and Tohlee to talk about Anoo and Eli and Jed about one of Jed's favorite topics—how the world ended up in the shape it did.

"We've talked about this before but let's start at the beginning, Jed," Eli suggests.

"The beginning is probably how people never stopped wanting more and more."

"More and more people wanted more and more," says Eli.

"Yes, population growth was not held back at a global level. Some people chose to have no or fewer babies, some countries tried to limit how many children its citizens could have, but global population growth was basically unaffected," says Jed.

"All those people wanted more and more for themselves and their children," says Eli.

"People saw what others had through social media and wanted those things for themselves. Things like cars for everyone, stable electrical sources, clean water, and high-quality medical care."

"So, not necessarily bad things or things based on greed or excess. It's that when everyone wants more and more, limits will be found in natural resources when a population is numbered in the billions."

"Consider an animal the size of a human with a population numbering in the billions. Looking at animal size—what's the largest animal that has that high of a population?" asks Jed.

"I guess I'm not sure. There aren't billions of blue whales or elephants certainly. Are there billions of deer?" Eli answers his own question. "If there are it's all the species in the world, not just one, and you'd probably have to include the various antelopes of Africa to actually raise the number up into the billions."

"I'd say the same with cattle. All the different types together might end up numbering in the billions yet not as many as the billions of people that wanted more and more. I'd guess you'd have to go to some songbird species to find the next largest animal with as many numbers in one species as humans had," says Jed.

"Okay, humans were the largest single animal species with the highest population and everyone wanted more and more. That drive for more and more caused resources to become depleted."

"That's right. Trees were cut down and deserts grew; ice caps melted and oceans rose; living soil was depleted as the variability of food plants diminished. Oceans warmed and acidified, causing them to be less productive. Water became more polluted and so more expensive to treat, which limited drinking water. People had to move away from rising ocean levels and growing deserts. They had to move to places where there already wasn't enough for everyone let alone enough for everyone to have more and more," says Jed.

"And that caused conflict," says Eli.

"Yes, people moved, people starved, and people killed. All the age-old divisions—racial, religious, national, and economic—erupted in violence against each other. There had been no true change in people since the century before when millions were exterminated for perceived differences. No change in people that could keep rationality, reason, and perspective strong and alive in the face of cold, hunger, violence, and privation. No change in people that could end the many thousands of years-long pattern of humanity spending its future on war," says Jed.

"Humanity has a long history of using violence to conquer excellence. A long history of one group taking what another has grown or made to benefit itself," says Eli and continues after a thoughtful pause, "usually resulting in no one having that developed excellence that was coveted in the first place."

"Some countries, like this one, used a disproportionate amount of world resources to benefit itself," says Jed.

"Taking away opportunities for others."

"This country chose to be dependent on cheap Middle Eastern oil to defeat the Soviet Union in their Cold War."

"A Cold War…with battles like Korea and Vietnam it wasn't very cold," says Eli and adds, "The Cold War conflict was worldwide; it just didn't happen all at the same time."

"The choice to be dependent on cheap Middle Eastern oil and the resultant use of military force to defend that dependency caused this country to exert a strong level of control over Middle Easterners' lives. A level of control that never would have been tolerated by this country if it was focused here by another country. That choice of dependency caused this Country of Freedom to have terrorism directed at it. That dependency was portrayed as a business deal. The terrorism was portrayed as coming from Muslims due to their religion. This predominantly Christian country, government, and military saw the Muslims as a threat because of its chosen dependency on Middle Eastern oil. Muslims saw this predominantly Christian country as a threat to their religion and way of life because of physical intrusions into their countries. The resulting conflict fed on age-old differences which created conflict between people like dwindling resources did," says Jed.

"This country ultimately lost its Cold World War because of the choices it made to temporarily win it. Cold War reverberations split apart all the age-old differences in a world stressed by numbers of people. Differences at a level of deep identity. Identity found in organized religion or nationalities or in a financial system are inherently vulnerable compared to identity found in the ability to determine individual perspective," says Eli.

"It took a half a century for the resultant turmoil to quiet down. Not because of an increase in tolerance and a drive to share and work together, but because the numbers of people had fallen and the energy to move large numbers of people vast distances to make war was scarce. People were having such a hard time surviving where they were they could no longer afford to wield military power to take from others who had barely enough for themselves. It was then that people began to reflect on what they had done to themselves, why they did it, and what could have been. They began to build instead of destroy. They began to learn that no matter which deity was watching, they were the ones acting. They realized that no ethereal being, nor a technologically advanced species from light-years away, had descended to Earth to deliver humanity to a promised land in their time of turmoil," says Jed.

"Now we have a Country of Freedom where there is virtually no national government. There are city-states that control the areas nearby that are useful for food and energy production. The governing power of some of these city-states can reach along corridors as much as a hundred miles to protect their energy sources and water. None of this power is used to administer laws and redistribute wealth beyond city control. The turmoil swallowed people of quality and good character as completely as the people who found truth in greed, violence, and conformity. And now, we have more individuals trying. Trying to grow compassion, not wealth. Trying to find unity, not division. Trying to feel tolerance, not enmity," says Eli.

Chapter Five

THE NEXT MORNING Anoo and Laurel greet each other with a full-body hug and a long, deep kiss. After stepping back and looking each other in the eye while holding hands Anoo gestures to the west. Laurel leads as they walk off into the woods. They walk through aspen groves large and small and meadows rocky and lush. It isn't hot yet and they are enjoying being together. They test each other's knowledge of the flowers and birds they see. Seeing some very large ponderosas they measure them with wraparound hugs. When animals go by, they watch without disturbing them until the animals move off on their own. At the edge of one meadow Laurel stops and Anoo steps up next to her. She drops down to the ground and then lays down on her belly. Looking up she gestures for Anoo to do the same. They imagine themselves small. Bunch grass becomes a thicket reaching over their heads. A purple aster flower bobbing on the end of its green stalk, a moving dinner plate for a bee. Laurel puts her head down and with Anoo they sniff the rich loam. They both think of the taste of Jerusalem artichokes and then they move into the soil. They are worms moving through the soil. Their entire bodies surrounded by food. What could be better than this, to be surrounded by food? Only a cool, moist night when they come up on the surface to have their entire bodies breathe. Oh! What could be better than having your entire body breathe? Finding a friend to share their rings of life with, coupling on a cool, moist night. Each one blissfully unaware of the robin the next day. Triangular beak piercing through the ceiling of their home. Squeezing and pulling with unimaginable strength as the worm strains. The hairs on its body pushing out against the walls of its home. So strong a pressure it can't resist any longer and the worm is in the belly of the beast. Then, high up on a branch above its home, what is left of it is pooped out to become the living soil the worm's future selves will be surrounded by. Now Laurel and Anoo are mice moving through the pliant, trembling stalks of grass that rise over their heads. They try not to cause the stalks to quiver with their movement as they approach a great big hole in the ground. It's bigger around than they are. They smell the winter home of a pocket gopher. They think about the home. A living room, toilet, and granary built out of solid ground. They don't go in. They haven't been invited. They move through the grass and there in front of them they find a big mouthful. A big mouthful of grass seed. It's in their mouths, filling their mouths with deliciously sweet nutty oil and protein. They're moving again when the earth shakes. Their world is moving up and down. Terrified with not knowing they shrink to the ground and hold on. The bounding fawn stops and looks at the two still bodies in its meadow. Stretching its neck toward the odd things it smells people. Suddenly the ground is quaking again for the mice and then the disturbance fades away. Quietly, subtly, the mice move on. They don't want to bring on the shadow. The blindingly fast shadow that will pierce them with horribly sharp talons and take them unimaginably high up into the brilliant blue.

Laurel and Anoo turn over. How can the world have so much blue? It surrounds them, everywhere, everywhere but on the periphery where lines of green stalks wave at them. Then they are chipmunks. Oh, to be so quick. Darting here and there. Daring to go out on a flexible but incredibly strong serviceberry stem. So strong under them until a gentle breeze bobs them up and down. They keep going and in front of them is purple. A purple bag too big to swallow whole. They sink their teeth into the berry and are rewarded with an explosion of purple goodness mixed with little crunches of seeds. It tastes so good! Now they are rabbits, timidly, cautiously, looking around and sniffing the air. Tasting here and tasting there. So much variety to try. They choose a favorite taste and indulge. Green wetness quenching their thirst and making their bodies strong. So strong they run across their meadow home and turn at full speed, darting here and there. This world of their meadow. So bright and warm they wish they could stay. It's time to hide. Time to put a roof of branches over their heads and rechew the morning's bounty. Now they're coyotes. Looking out from under tall shrubs at the edge of the meadow. Where can they go and pounce? Here? Or should they run across the meadow to the shade of the aspen? Where to most efficiently spend their energy? Their energy so hard-earned it must be used wisely. They have enough though. Enough to joyously run with their family from one meadow to another and to howl with delight when one makes a kill. Enough to howl at the sheer pleasure of coming home to their burrow with a full belly.

Laurel and Anoo turn over and look up into the blue. They feel the solid earth under them as they breathe in life-sustaining air. Then they're up in that blue as birds. Muscles straining, wings lifting them up. With their speed the air is almost as thick as a liquid. They feel it as a flexible moving base they can use to shift direction as they see an insect to feed on. They need so many insects. So many to keep them up here. So many to move them a world away to avoid the insect desert of winter. Laurel and Anoo's hands touch. They give each other a squeeze and hold on for a few minutes. They get up and walk. After a short wander they hear crows being very raucous a little way away. Laurel looks at Anoo and he smiles with a "who knows" look and gestures toward the sound. As they get closer they see the crows moving away and their calls stop. A few minutes later they hear the squawk of an upset robin from the same place the crows were. Now that they are near the robin they move forward slowly and quietly. It sounds like another robin has joined in. They can see the robins moving around an aspen branch but can't see what they're interested in through the leaves. Another few steps and they see a great horned owl stoically sitting on the branch. The robins are squawking and dive-bombing the owl. It's pretending not to notice but they can see it flinch when the robins peck. See the disturbed feathers where the pecks have landed. After watching a while the robins decide they're hungrier than they are upset with the owl and move off. A minute later the owl gives his feathers a shake, smoothing out the roughing-up the feathers took from the robins. Anoo and Laurel slip away and find a shady spot to sit.

"That was fun to see," says Laurel. "Why do you think the owl put up with all that? It could have just left."

"Maybe it just fledged last month or so and isn't very comfortable moving around," suggests Anoo. "It found a place it thought it could safely spend the day and didn't want to leave."

"That's a very reasonable possibility spoken by a very reasonable man. Let's hear some more of your thinking on things. You choose the topic."

"Okay, how about vagueness?" asks Anoo.

"The devil is in the details, so to speak," replies Laurel.

"That's the saying. We don't have to consider a devil that influences physical reality to discuss the concept. We can use the saying to represent individual acts of evil or dishonorable value systems."

"Dishonorable value systems?" asks Laurel.

"An egotist who thinks their lies are better than the truth. A person who thinks successfully deceiving others is a statement of their wisdom. An ugly person who thinks anger validates perspective."

"That's a definition I can work with," says Laurel.

"So how did you get from vagueness to details?" asks Anoo.

"The devil is in vagueness. It only shows that the devil has been there all along when one looks at details," explains Laurel.

"I like that, go on."

"Instead of the devil we could say lies, deceit, false perspectives are in vagueness."

"Okay, I think I'm following," says Anoo. "A vague statement can contain negative factors. Those negative factors could repudiate the perspective that was presented vaguely if the negative factors were presented clearly."

"Yes, thank you. Clear and concise statements like you just gave can't be used to weasel one's way out of responsibility for an error in perspective like vagueness can. I think clearly proving one's points and so taking responsibility for one's perspective is a very mature way to interact with others."

"Proving one's points gives the opportunity for listeners to assess what's being said at their own pace using their own experiences. Accepting responsibility through clear statements includes accepting error in one's statements. That acceptance of error keeps self-righteous ego at bay," says Anoo.

"Proving one's points allows the listener the opportunity to rise above 'don't think—obey' to deciding for themselves. Self-righteous ego is inherently a false path to follow. Did we get to this point already?"

"Yes. At least the rising above 'don't think—obey.' That was when we were talking about conclusions based on feelings."

"I remember, Anoo, and I think this fits right in. Vagueness allows for deceitful tricks, self-serving manipulations, or propaganda based on catchwords and catchphrases. Proof of perspective based on clear statements creates the opportunity for a listener to rise above the inherent negativity of 'don't think—obey.'"

"Well stated, Laurel. And that gets me thinking of the idea of using 'I,' when it's fitting, instead of lumping oneself into a group."

"Give me an example. It does sound like the lumping into a group is vagueness and using 'I' would be more defined and so have more clarity."

"I think that's how I got to this point in our conversation," says Anoo. "To use coarse generalities to make a point I'll consider a woman who says women can't think like an engineer. They feel instead. Or a man who says he can't understand empathy because he's a man. Because he's a man he needs to have the circumstances explained."

"You're saying an individual shouldn't blame their inability on gender, or age, or circumstance. They should confront the perceived inability in themselves," restates Laurel.

"Yes, hiding inability behind gender takes away from the opportunity to grow above the inability."

"While at the same time demeaning the gender by taking away from woman engineers and, I'll say, male doctors who need to empathize with patients to understand their symptoms," adds Laurel.

"It's the equivalent of saying you can't do that because you're a girl," says Anoo. "It's a pile of defeatism like 'you can't fight city hall' or don't think about the truth of my perceptive feelings, just agree with them. Which is a derivative of 'don't think—obey.'"

"You just covered the negative generality of 'my feelings are the truth' with your statement 'don't think about the truth of my perceptive feelings, just agree with them,' but you didn't get at the underlying perspective."

"Please explain," Anoo encourages.

"My feelings are the truth," restates Laurel. "What perspective is the individual basing this statement on? Their feelings are a universal truth, so agree or you're wrong. Another way to look at those kind of feelings is that my feelings are my individual truth based on my perspective, my experiences, and my current understanding of the issue at hand. If I learn a new piece of information my feelings could change."

"'My feelings are the truth' would be the vagueness where error may reside. The generality that hides one's inability to prove their point, or the inability to understand one's perspective well enough to explain it to others. 'My feelings are my own individual truth' is a clear statement that the individual is taking responsibility for their perspective and is willing to learn about the subject the feelings are based on," concludes Anoo.

"Whew! I've enjoyed this conversation, Anoo. I want a definition of perceptive feelings and then I think it will be time for a walk."

"Perceptive feelings would be how people assess other people, or concepts, or a person's actions with their subconscious mind."

"That sounds a lot like intuition."

"I think intuition would be a comparable term," replies Anoo. "Maybe the person having the feeling is using small body language tips as cues. Maybe they're getting information through an empathetic connection. The idea is that the feeling isn't the result of conscious thought by the person getting the feeling or a blatant statement by the person being assessed."

"Okay, I think I'm following you. Let's go for a walk."

Not far along they drop into a steep ravine. It runs roughly south to north. The east-facing side is thick with ponderosas, fir, and some lodgepole. The west-facing side is more open but still well vegetated with large juniper and a scattering of very large ponderosas. Along the little stream at the bottom is thick grass surrounding tall blue spruce and some willow. They look at each other like the place is magical and slowly walk along the stream holding hands when they can. At a small boggy area next to the stream they find a patch of late-blooming, dark red paintbrush mixed with bog orchids. They watch for a while as the flowers have attracted an assortment of bees and flies. They hear some more squeaking and squawking but it doesn't sound like birds this time. It sounds more like chattering. Moving slowly uphill toward the sound they hear the chattering grow louder, quiet, and start up again. Soon they see two long shapes chasing each other in a large ponderosa. It's two pine marten and they look like they're playing. Anoo and Laurel watch the game of tag, marveling at the animals' agility and ability to grip the tree bark. After enjoying the sounds of the martens chattering and their claws scratching bark Anoo and Laurel go back down to the stream. They stop at a little pool, take off their shoes, and soak their feet.

"Do you think they're friends, or siblings?" asks Laurel.

"I think that was foreplay," says Anoo.

"Isn't it too soon for foreplay? Wouldn't they have their young in the spring? The best time to find enough food to grow babies. They're too small for a full winter-long gestation like deer and elk. Let alone gestation starting around the end of summer."

"They will mate now, or soon; then the female delays implantation of the fertilized eggs until spring," answers Anoo.

"Hmmm, an interesting adaptation. My feet are getting cold. Let's move over to that log and sit a while."

After drying their feet, they relax against the downed tree trunk. Anoo looks at Laurel.

"Your mother stays at winter camp?"

"My grandfather and our people raised me. My father left on a hunting and exploring trip when I was four and never returned. My mother thinks he left her. Grandfather thinks something sudden happened to him or he'd have sensed a problem."

"He was your grandfather's son?"

"My mother is Grandfather's daughter. Grandfather and my father knew each other well. I'm sure that's why Grandfather thinks he'd have sensed a developing concern."

"And your mother?"

"She never got over his not coming back. She doesn't leave winter camp and has been very distant with everyone since. I was mostly raised by the other mothers and my grandfather."

"And your grandmother, Grandfather's wife?"

"I never knew her. She passed a few years before I was born."

"That all sounds like it would have been hard for you."

"Not as much as you might think. I had several women in an aunt type of position and a couple grandmother substitutes too. There were also several girls roughly my age, which helped."

Anoo isn't sure what to say after that and Laurel doesn't seem to want to talk. After a few minutes, "Laurel, I want to hold you. Would you turn more facing me?"

She swivels around until she is sitting facing him. He puts his arms around her and pulls her down toward his chest. They adjust a little until Laurel is curled up with her head on Anoo's chest and his arms are wrapped around her. Once again, she relaxes within the loving arms of a friend.

After a short time their legs and backs start to feel like it's time to move. Laurel sits up. Her heart is feeling warm from Anoo's embrace. She looks him in the eye and kisses him. "Thank you," she says. They stand and stretch until they loosen up and then walk along the stream again. It's early afternoon and it doesn't take much walking to feel warm. They stop next to the stream in the shade of a large spruce. There's a little gravel bar above the low water of August with a nice rock to lean against. Laurel motions Anoo to sit. He leans back against the rock and Laurel sits between his legs. Leaning against his chest she takes his hands and puts them on her breasts. Anoo kisses several of her braids one by one and then enjoys the feel of her womanly body. Laurel moves his hands to her stomach and hugs them to her.

"I want to talk about how you're feeling about us becoming a couple, Anoo."

"Okay, but I need to move."

"Oh! Did I sit on you?"

"No, I just need to straighten myself up."

"There you are, Anoo. It's nice to feel you."

Remembering and laughing Anoo replies, "You were just feeling me."

"But I'm feeling more of you now." Laurel laughs. "Now that I have you right where I want you... Are we becoming a couple?"

"Each day we're together I feel like I want more. More talk, more touch, more sharing our time here on this beautiful mysterious planet. More sharing with you in this magnificent experiment called life. And obviously, as you can feel, I want to share our bodies' ability to give pleasure."

"Let's just say tomorrow for that, Anoo. Right now, I want to talk about what we're going to do when we join and we become a couple like I'm hoping we will."

"Okay, first, I want tomorrow to be the day for us. Tomorrow I don't want our joining day to become tomorrow again. I know we have the day after too. I want that day to be a growing as a coupling couple day."

"I like the feel of your hard bargain. Decision made. What are we going to do if I want you every day like I want you tomorrow?"

"We could still decide to spend the winter apart. Ow! That finger is supposed to be attached to my hand, Laurel!"

"Start your options again or it won't be for long."

"We could be together at the farm or at winter camp."

"Pluses and minuses?"

"I've been wanting a change. Harvest time is not a time I can leave my parents' farm though. They need help to secure the bounty of the season's work."

"How long will harvest take?"

"Most is done by October. There's still some to do when we get back from hunting in November. Like digging the potatoes and carrots that we didn't get to earlier before the ground freezes. That just means getting them out of the ground and into the root cellar though. The most help is needed with preparing and preserving the variety of produce we grow. Shaving corn off the ear for drying for example. The great majority of that work is done before we go hunting and I wouldn't need to be around for the later finish-up work. You guys leave for winter camp around mid-September? That's not much time for me to help with the harvest."

"Mid-September is when we start to move the sheep back. It takes a couple weeks. Several of the guys stay up here longer to move more loads of wood for the winter. Their last trip isn't until around the middle of October. Their last few trips include taking some deer and elk besides the wood to winter camp."

"So, we could go to the farm and help with harvest until at least early October. Meet up with the guys for a final hunt and wood cutting, then we'd travel to winter camp with them. With your help harvesting at the farm, that could work."

"Let's think about that some. You talk to Mateen and I'll talk to Grandfather. Right now, I need to get up. Because this," Laurel says, while sitting up a little and rubbing her butt against Anoo, "feels too good."

"Oh! Laurel!" says Anoo while pulling her tight against him. "I wasn't prepared for that kind of touching!"

"Let me up, Anoo," Laurel says, laughing. "I want more of our growing together before we join."

"Tomorrow," finishes Anoo.

They walk farther down the stream to where it splits a small grassy meadow. A steep east-facing slope shades the meadow from the harshest of the afternoon sun's rays, causing the meadow to be green and inviting. As they walk around the meadow they stop at a scattering of flicker feathers. Anoo picks up a dozen of the brightest-colored ones. Going to the stream he first trims off the frilly parts at the base and then washes the feathers off. Laurel smiles as he steps up to her. She turns slowly while Anoo works them one by one into her braids. When she's facing him again she puts her hands around his neck and pulls him in for a long kiss. Smiling, she starts walking down the stream again. At one point, just above the stream, they see a bench with serviceberry and chokecherry shrubs covering it. Both types of shrub still have berries. After enjoying the flavor of the serviceberries alternating with the tartness of the chokecherries they have a chokecherry pit spitting contest. Anoo thinks he won with an exceptionally long spit. Laurel thinks the spit should be disqualified due to the benefit of an extra strong breeze. Not really caring they take a break on a grassy spot mostly shaded by the shrubs. Anoo takes a small blanket out of his pack and rolls it into a long pillow. Lying down next to each other they relax. After a short nap Laurel sees if Anoo is awake by moving her foot next to his and pushing down. Anoo pulls up with his foot. Looking up at the sky they both smile. Anoo sits up and reaches into his pack and pulls out a bag of raisins. He lies back, resting up on an elbow, and takes a raisin from the bag. He places it on Laurel's lips and she promptly eats it and then another. Then Anoo takes a raisin and runs it all around

Laurel's lips before giving it to her. He reaches up and runs his finger over each of her eyebrows. Putting his finger between them he runs it down her nose to her lips. As he lightly runs his finger over her lips she feels an extra little tickle and her tongue darts out touching his finger. Anoo puts another raisin against her lips but as she tries to take it into her mouth he pulls it back and eats it himself. Then he reaches down and puts his fingers on the top button of her sleeveless blouse. He looks at her and she smiles. He undoes the button and gives her a raisin. Another button and another raisin until all the buttons are undone. He slowly opens her blouse and looks at her breasts. Taking out another raisin he runs it around her areola and reaches up and feels her lips again on his fingertips as she takes it into her mouth. He does the same with her other breast and then two raisins for him delightfully flavored the same way. Next, he puts a raisin by her nipple and, smiling, he looks her in the eye. She smiles back. He bends down and sucks the raisin and her nipple into his mouth. She gives a little gasp and he slowly chews the raisin while looking at her beautiful smiling face. He does the same to her other nipple. Suddenly Laurel sits up and squeezes his hardness and then quickly gets to her feet.

"I can't take any more of this, Anoo. We have to walk some more!"

"Oh! You naughty tease!"

"Me? You're the tease and guilty of bribery by raisin besides!"

"I fully admit to being guilty as charged," admits Anoo, laughing.

"I only squeezed you to see if you're as aroused as I am," explains Laurel.

"I want to feel how aroused you are too."

"You'll have to take my word for it today. I can assure you, in my own way, I am. Even though my arousal isn't as out front and noticeable as yours."

Standing in front of him with her blouse still open and smiling she adds, "Well, except for these. Anoo, I want you to know, if a relationship between us works out the way I want it to and the way I'm feeling it will, we'll be equals. I'm an innie, you're an outie and

'Viva la Difference.' I won't think you'll owe me something because I'm an innie."

"Owe you?"

"I won't use my innie as a unit of barter with you. For example, I won't ever expect you to consider my feelings in our relationship a greater truth than yours in exchange for your opportunity to indulge in my innie."

"I understand. And to you, Laurel, I will never expect to get my way in our relationship based on any factor but a full explanation and then acceptance from you. If we both explain our positions and we can't come to terms, then 'Viva la Difference' as individuals as well as genders."

"If we can't come to terms will we ask your uncle or my grandfather their advice as the oldest most experienced people around?"

"If we need to ask anyone my parents are more likely the ones with the most experience making a couple's relationship work. And now, if I'm going to be comfortable walking, I need to button you back up."

Anoo steps up to Laurel and buttons the lowest button of her blouse. Laurel reaches up and puts her arms around Anoo's neck. Anoo buttons the next button and they kiss. Another button and another kiss. After the last button Anoo says, "Well, that didn't work. I guess we're just going to have to start walking to get my mind off how arousing you are."

After walking most of the way back to their meeting place Laurel and Anoo take a break. Lying on their pillow again they decide to talk more.

"You pick a topic, Laurel."

"Okay, working off the earlier idea of who to ask for advice. Is the oldest person's perspective or feelings the most accurate? Do they contain the most truth?"

"Different people do not learn the same things at the same time. Learning is an individual process dependent more on intent than age," explains Anoo.

"If the oldest person's perspective is looked at as containing the most truth what would happen if that person left the room?" asks Laurel.

"I guess truth would shift to the next oldest person, requiring truth to be more nebulous than I see it as from my individual perspective."

"If an older person then walked into the room?" continues Laurel.

"Truth would shift again, proving how ridiculous the concept is in the first place."

"Give me an example of when people seek out the oldest person for their opinion on a particular topic."

"I guess I can't think of any. If I needed advice, I'd seek out the person who knew the most about whatever topic I was dealing with as we were saying earlier about my parents and relationships," Anoo concludes.

"Give me a topic connected with life in general where people seek out the oldest person's opinion," prompts Laurel.

"I still can't think of any. General topics don't need specific wisdom," answers Anoo.

"Would you seek out the oldest person's opinion for questions about life?" asks Laurel.

"I think the term *life* is a vague statement which hides a flaw in perspective. As soon as the term *life* is defined as something specific I would ask a person who has chosen to learn about that particular aspect of life what their perspective is and I would expect them to prove their point. For example, there's the saying that there are two things people can't avoid in life—death and taxes. If I needed advice about taxes I'd ask a person who has tried to learn about taxes, not the oldest person around. I'm not sure how I'd make the same argument about death, so I'll switch to illness. If I was ill I'd seek out a doctor to help me determine the problem, not the oldest person around."

"I know you're just making a point, but do you guys have taxes?" wonders Laurel.

"There's a tax for the electricity that is produced by the town's power plant. It can't be a set fee because there is no way to measure use by household. Do you guys have taxes?"

"We usually barter, so we don't have taxes on transactions. We do pay a fee for schooling in town. It's based on how many kids are going. Okay, let's go to who's smarter, men or women?" asks Laurel.

"The individual who finds the least amount of truth in generalities like 'men are this' or 'women are that' is the smartest."

"Who are the people that find truth in generalities?" asks Laurel.

"People who haven't defined the value systems they perceive the world through, people who perceive the world and others through generalities, people who find more truth in the average than in the exception."

"What does a person who has intentionally defined their value systems feel when someone tries to categorize them within generalities?" Laurel continues.

"Like their efforts at defining their individuality aren't being appreciated."

"A person who has made the effort to define themselves tries to treat the people around them as individuals because…?" asks Laurel.

"The golden rule. That's how that individual wants to be treated."

"When there is the possibility of a relationship, but one person treats the other through generalities the one being treated through generalities thinks?" prompts Laurel.

"A guy will think, *May as well see if I can have sex with this girl because I wouldn't want a relationship with her.* What will a girl think?"

"*This guy is a waste of my time.* I like our little speed rounds, Anoo."

"I like talking to you, walking with you, lying down and relaxing with you. Laurel, I can't imagine anyone else I'd rather be sharing the experience of falling in love with."

"Thank you for saying so, Anoo. And I feel the same towards you. Have you ever felt like tomorrow will never come?"

"You mean besides now?" sighs Anoo with a smile.

"Do you just want to join right now?"

"Yes. Do you?"

"Absolutely. Should we?"

"I guess not."

"Poop. But you're the man, so you're always right."

"Hey! wait a second!" Anoo says, laughing. "So, now if I say let's just do it, the man won't always be right. The only way I'll be right is if we don't do it now. You trickster."

"I just couldn't pass up the opportunity," Laurel says, laughing.

With that Anoo rolls on top of Laurel. Both laughing, Laurel lifts her knees, spreads her legs, and Anoo lets his weight settle on her. Then, looking into each other's eyes.

"Tomorrow, Laurel."

"Tomorrow, Anoo. With my open heart, my hopes for a future with you, my desire for you, my newfound love for you."

"Tomorrow, Laurel. With my desire to share our lives together, my desire to be a better person for you, my desire to make your life better for you. I'm falling in love with you, Laurel."

"I'm falling in love with you too, Anoo."

After walking back to their meeting place the couple have a little time and decide to talk more. Sitting down next to each other with their shoulders touching Laurel takes Anoo's hand in hers.

"You pick a topic, Anoo."

"I do have a topic I've been wanting to bring up," says Anoo. "I want to talk about the seeming distinctions between heart and mind, body and soul, reason and feelings."

"Your hands are very strong. I shouldn't be surprised as farming is about as literally a hands-on occupation as a person can have. Go ahead, I'm a little distracted in a nice way but I'm listening."

"I think the distinctions that can seem so real between heart and mind, body and soul, reason and feelings should be brought together, not emphasized."

"How so?" Laurel brings Anoo's hand up to her mouth and kisses each of his knuckles.

"I think that those seemingly different concepts, found in each of us, function best when working together."

"How so?" asks Laurel as she puts Anoo's hand on her knee and her hand on the inside of his elbow and pulls his upper arm against her breast.

"I think that those pairs of concepts, when working together, become greater than the sum of their parts."

"How so?" Laurel takes her hand from his elbow and slides it down his inner thigh.

"Laurel! This is not having a conversation."

"I think I'm saying a lot."

"That's not what I mean!"

"I know, Anoo," says Laurel, laughing. "I understand what you're saying. Those pairs aren't meant to work separately. They're meant to be in a symbiotic relationship like the algae and fungus that make up a lichen. The two parts together become more than the sum of their parts. I was being the inefficiency that causes the pair of us not to work well together as a couple. I want us to be the algae and the fungus that take a likin' to each other to become a lichen."

"You really are a remarkable person, Laurel."

"We are getting to know each other, aren't we?" asks Laurel, still laughing. "And how can you be smiling and look exasperated at the same time?"

"I guess I need to use my mind's understanding of what you just did to bring my feelings together."

"I'm taking a likin' to you, Anoo."

"I like you and am impressed by you, Laurel."

"Good, okay, I'll keep going. Hearts and minds need to work

together. They can no more be separate than hearts can live without the brain or the brain live without the heart. Thoughts and feelings—feelings need to be tempered with thoughtful communication and learning to increase the accuracy of the feelings. Thought without heart is logic. The patterns make sense but don't have meaningful application without the usefulness of added heart. Body and soul—the soul needs the body to grow itself. The body needs soul for meaning to life. What do you think?"

"I think I'm in over my head and I like it."

"Then, I think it's time for me to go."

After saying a long, warm, affectionate good-bye Anoo walks back to the cabin. When he gets there, he finds it empty. He steps out the front door and hears knocking in the distance. Walking in that direction he finds Mateen chopping up a tree. Mateen turns and waves just before Anoo calls out hello to avoid any possibility of an accident. Even with the concentration needed for chopping and the resultant noise Mateen has sensed him drawing near. Seeing lengths of trunk small enough for him to handle alone Anoo starts making trips back to the cabin. Then he takes over chopping for a while as Mateen takes a break. They stack the wood they're leaving so it won't get wet sitting on the ground and make a last carry back to the cabin. After showers, they sit on the front porch looking into the aspen stand. The sun is low enough to be partially covered by trees, and shadows are long.

"Let's have a serious discussion before dinner, Anoo."

"Okay, connected to a relationship?"

"No, connected to what divides people in the most profound way."

"Dividing people like being a follower or a creator?" asks Anoo, remembering their conversation a few days ago.

"This is similar but different."

"So, a dividing factor other than religion, appearance, or economic status?" asks Anoo.

"That's right. The division is where does an individual find truth? Does the individual look for truth in themselves or outside themselves? For the most part people who look for truth outside themselves are followers and people who look for truth in themselves are creators."

"Does that depend on the truth one is looking for?"

"Maybe, we'll see where we end up. I'm thinking that for at least the great majority of situations it won't matter. I'll start with a comparison. I think people who look for truth in themselves end up deciding truth is based on their own value systems, experiences, and their resultant perspective."

"Those truths can then change through the process of learning, changing, and growing," Anoo adds to show he's following.

"Yes, and because of that process people who look for truth inside themselves have tolerance for other people's perspective. They understand another individual is in a learning process also. That individual's value systems and experiences may point them to another perspective of truth that is different from theirs but not wrong."

"As long as they are applying 'do unto others,' not committing acts of violence, not deceiving others for their own gain, among others concerns," Anoo qualifies.

"That's right. Now let's look at the other side of this. At individuals who look for truth outside themselves. They may look for truth in an authority figure like the leader of a country or a religion, or in the hierarchy of a corporation, or the military. They may seek truth in a political party or an individual considered wise, a guru, a sage, a bodhisattva, the leader of a cult. They may look for truth outside themselves in a book a religion is based on or a building where people with similar religious perspectives go to worship. By their choice of where to find truth those people limit their growth as individuals. They do more to grow the structure they are finding truth in with their numbers than grow their own individual truth."

"Any and all of those particulars can be used as an information source to cause learning, change, and growth. That process of growth needs to be incorporated into individual perspective to be valid. Following does not lead to efficient individual growth, nor does massing together lead to truth," states Anoo.

"What does following those particulars lead to?" asks Mateen and answers himself. "Looking for truth in the leader of a country leads to authoritarianism and then fascism or dictatorship. Finding truth in a political party leads to head-butting confrontation. Someone who finds truth in a religious leader or a religion will find themselves becoming a fanatic and can end up being led into a religious war. Find truth in a military structure and of course you'll end up in a war. A wise man, fanaticism again, and self-delusion. A corporation, greed. I'll put books and buildings into subsets under my stated examples. Truth is not democratic. The largest organization is not the truth. A democratic country's goal should be the most freedom for the most individuals so those individuals can gain the most from their individual path of learning, change, and growth. Organizing people through nationalism or religious truth causes divisions in humanity because of the numbers of country's and religions. Divisions that can be exploited by authority figures or causes. Divisions that inhibit the application of tolerance to others on an individual level. What are the tools of people who seek to divide?"

"Hate, racial inequality, the declaration of religious truth, economic disparity, restriction of freedom of the press and speech," replies Anoo.

"Well answered. Individual determination of truth leads to compassion for others and an understanding of the effort they are making. Following other's truths leads to intolerance. I think our conversation has worked up as much of an appetite for me as chopping wood did." Mateen smiles.

During dinner Anoo tells Mateen about his plans with Laurel. Her helping with the harvest and then both going to winter camp. They agree it would be a good way for Laurel to meet Anoo's parents and to get the farm work done before Anoo leaves for the winter. Mateen says to stay at the cabin on their way to the farm. After a short pause Mateen says Grandfather will accompany Laurel to the cabin and then stay and visit for a few days.

Chapter Six

EACH MORNING LAUREL and Anoo have met a little earlier. Each day together has been long enough for their newfound feelings for each other to grow. Each morning their greeting hug has been a firmer embrace. Their greeting kiss longer, deeper, and more passionate. This morning's even more so as they look into each other's eyes.

"Good morning, Anoo."

"Good morning, Laurel. It's very nice to see you again."

"It warms my heart to see you walking up to me, Anoo."

Stepping back, they hold each other's hands.

"Laurel, the morning sun on your face is the most beautiful sight I've ever seen."

"Anoo, your hug, your kiss, lets me feel myself whole in a way I've never felt before."

"Laurel."

"Okay, we know each other's name...Anoo."

"Okay...Laurel," Anoo says, laughing. "What should we do today? I'm thinking of something."

"Is it a walk and a talk like our other beautiful days together?"

"If we're naked."

"Today is yesterday's tomorrow all day; let's get naked a little later."

"I'd like very much to walk and talk with you, Laurel."

They don't walk very far. This morning their being together is enough of a journey. They find a nice place to sit and look for a while. They're on the upper side of a gently sloping meadow. It's not very far to the bottom edge or the right side. To the left the meadow wraps out of sight around the hill they're sitting on. The sun is climbing in the sky behind them.

"Should we talk about our sharing our lives together?" asks Anoo.

"Let's talk about the freedoms we'll be living our lives with."

"You're saying *freedoms* with emphasis."

"I mean speech, press, religion, peaceable assembly, and petitioning grievances," states Laurel.

"Okay, you start."

"These freedoms are a legal right under this country's constitution. This Country of Freedom. The right to be free from governmental oppression in these areas. These freedoms can also be lived on an individual level."

"I agree completely; please continue," Anoo encourages.

"They can be lived by every man, woman, and child, of every race, color, religion, or any other category."

"The Founding Fathers were fully aware of the various peoples, races, and religions on this great broad earth. They meant for this country to be inclusive, not divisive. For this country to be a haven of freedom for all Homo sapiens," says Anoo.

"Thank you. Freedom of speech does not include the right to make others listen but does include hate speech and divisive speech."

"That's by definition," agrees Anoo. "At the same time those who engage in hate speech, or speech intended to cause division, do so from a corrupted heart and a flawed character, from their own inability to live American freedoms on an individual level."

"Individuals attempting to cause division between the people of this Country are going against the spirit of the Constitution. Their anger or willingness to do violence in the cause of divisiveness is un-American," states Laurel.

"People who think anger or violence validates perspective are actively proving the theory of evolution. They are individuals who are functioning on the level of grunting apes. My apologies to apes. I was only filling in. I want to hear more from you."

"Censorship is choosing not to read something, not preventing printing," continues Laurel.

"Censorship is an individual responsibility. By constitutional right it cannot be governmental responsibility," affirms Anoo.

"Freedom of religion includes all religions."

"The Founding Fathers used the word *God* knowing full well its definition is any monotheistic religion. Which at the very least includes the three religions based on the God of Abraham. Judaism, Christianity, and Islam," says Anoo.

"I'm sure there are more. Most religions considered by some to be pluralistic had a supreme being. They just have multiple levels between God and people," adds Laurel.

"Christianity has its hierarchy," says Anoo in support.

"The right to peaceably assemble does not include the right to carry weaponry while assembling," continues Laurel.

"Which does not infringe on the right to own such weaponry, only the use of such weaponry to validate perspective. Freely assembling while carrying weapons is the equivalent of hate speech or using anger to validate perspective. And is indicative of the same flawed character development we just talked about," Anoo explains, showing he's following.

"I'm almost done. There's petitioning grievances. If the grievance includes hate or anger or if intimidation is used to attempt to include others in the petition, the petition is as flawed as the individual's character. This country was founded on its Constitutional Freedoms, not the Ten Commandments, or the Bible, or Christian principles. A majority of people may have chosen those concepts as their right to freedom of choice. That majority of people do not have the right to limit the freedoms in the Constitution for others," concludes Laurel.

"Truth is not democratic. The voting process is. That's strong stuff, Laurel, and I applaud your conviction and agree in total with you. I also think we should take a walk."

Anoo helps Laurel up. After a long hug they walk down the length of the meadow. Out in the open, under the blue sky and bright sun, together, they hold hands. With Anoo on the downhill side of the gently sloping meadow they are equals. Equals in height, perspective, desire, and in hopes for the future. In a funny way, even the pocket gophers living in the meadow are contributing to their being together. The gopher's piles of excavated earth from the previous winter make for unsteady walking. Holding hands steadies them, links, strengthens, and unites them. Here, out in the meadow, they turn and look at each other. Anoo takes his pack off and takes out his little blanket. Laurel takes it from him and spreads it out. Turning back to Anoo she unbuttons her blouse and puts it in her carry bag. Sitting on the blanket she leans back on her elbows and looks up at Anoo.

"Just like this?" he asks.

"Like this but I want your pants off. I don't want to feel clothes between my legs."

Anoo takes his pants off as Laurel watches. He stands in front of her a little self-conscious. She only sees him straight and strong and proud. A physical representation of his character. Kneeling, Anoo watches as Laurel pulls up her skirt and more and more of her legs show. As her skirt reaches the top of her thighs he looks into her eyes. Leaning forward they touch, and he's deep inside her in a breath of time. He's enveloped by her and she's pushing up wanting more contact. Looking in each other's eyes they're feeling more than seeing. He's moving and then thrusting as Laurel is. Soon they're both laughing at their release and the overwhelming need that led them here.

"That's not exactly how I thought this would go," says Anoo with a smile.

"Our joining parts have been encouraged by the rest of us," answers Laurel.

"Encouraged?"

"Our joining parts were encouraged by the feel of our fingertips touching as we looked at a flower together. The feel of your hand and the strength in your arm as you helped me up that steep bank by the stream. That quick look of lust I saw on your face before I pushed you under the waterfall. My appreciation of your consideration as you meticulously cleaned up the flicker feathers you fixed in my hair. The delight my girlfriends expressed in the way the feathers' orange splashes of color went all the way around just a little more than half-way down my black braids. The laugh we shared when Briana said the last thing a guy put in her hair was a squirrel tail with the end still bloody."

Laughing, Anoo replies, "I see. My seeing your naked body under the full light of a bright sun. The feel of your lips on my fingertips as I fed you raisins. The beauty of your face when I wanted so much to kiss you but thought it too soon. I want to catch our joining parts up some more, Laurel."

"Please be back inside me, Anoo."

This time, it isn't the need for bodies to release passion that over-whelms them. It is Anoo's realization that he can go deeper into Laurel's eyes than he ever could be in her body. And Laurel's realiza-tion that she wants Anoo in her heart and life even more than her body wants his deep inside her.

They join with a breeze rustling through the grasses around them. With the sun touching their exposed skin. With hearts and minds and bodies.

Afterward, they finish undressing and lie down next to each other. After a short nap Laurel pushes her foot down on Anoo's. He pulls his up to show he's awake.

"I want to do it again, Anoo."

"I'm not quite ready."

"I'll help."

Laurel kneels next to Anoo and kisses his eyelids and his mouth. Kissing his throat she continues down to both his nipples. She lets her breasts slide over his chest and down his stomach. Then down past his waist to his far thigh. She continues back up and around and down his near thigh. Leaning forward she takes him into her mouth.

110

In a minute Anoo is ready again and Laurel stretches her leg over him and eases herself down. Under the warm sun, in this bright meadow, on rich fertile soil, Laurel says, "Let's talk some more."

"You don't mean philosophizing?"

"No, just talk. What do you want to talk about?"

"I really don't care at this point," Anoo admits.

"My choice then. How about preferred sexual positions?"

"Okay, I prefer whichever I'm doing at the time."

"That's like which flower do I like best? The ones that are blooming at my feet are my favorite. What situation goes with what position?" Laurel prods.

"I'm not sure what you mean. I don't have a problem with any position I've tried."

"As a future hint to you, me either. I'll go first. Say we have been living together for a while and you are away for a few days. When you come home I'd say the missionary position would be the way to go."

"I'm not following you."

"We'd race to the bedroom, I'd get naked, lie back on the bed, spread my legs, and say, 'Get that thing into me, Anoo, I missed you.' Then you'd give me an energetic thumping and we'd finish. No long, drawn-out affair. Your turn."

"I'm not sure how but you just gave me the urge to live with you and leave often."

"Good one, Anoo." Laurel laughs and repeats, "Your turn."

"Okay, I think I see how this works. How about doggie style is my favorite on a full moon night. Because doggie style isn't doggie style without some howling."

Laughing again Laurel says: "You've got it. Okay, my favorite sexual position after you've had an especially hard day farming is me on top like this. I'd work you up with my mouth and then sit on you like I just did. Then I'd grind away until I'd given you a good soaking. Your turn."

"I don't know what to say except I think I'm even harder."

"I think that counts as a forfeited turn. My favorite position on a hot summer afternoon would be spooning. That way you can fan me and feed me grapes."

"You may think that wouldn't appeal to me but you'd be wrong."

"Your turn," says Laurel.

"This might be a little different but my favorite position, just some of the time, not a particular time, is frog position."

"What's that? You behind me grabbing my boobs? Like a frog clutching his mate?"

"I'm behind you, you're flat on your stomach, with your legs together. My feet are up by your butt so my legs are way bent like a frog about to jump. Boobs aren't really involved."

"I got you. What am I doing though?" asks Laurel.

"Well, enjoying the many different twists and turns of my passion-filled lovemaking."

"I don't think that would be enough. I think I should get to read a book."

"A book! Excuse me."

"Sure, not something in-depth that takes a lot of concentration. Maybe a picture book."

"Oh, I don't believe it. I mean the most I would grant is the need for a pop-up book."

"Okay, I'll settle."

"Laurel?"

"Yes, Anoo?"

"It's not farming but I've been doing some hard work today."

Throwing her head back and laughing Laurel does as she said she would.

"I'm getting warm, Anoo."

"I'm getting too much sun on places that are usually covered, except for swimming of course. And walking sometimes. And drying off after an outdoor shower. I like to be naked."

"Me too. Let's go be naked together in the shade of those aspens."

A short walk across the meadow and they're in shade. They stop in a grassy spot with small patches of sun and spread out their blanket. Lying down they relax for a while. A few chickadees come by giving their chick-a-dee-dee-dee call. Anoo mimics the call with a kind of hissing inflection. The birds come closer as though they're feeling secure from the sound. They hunt and call all around the couple as Anoo continues his call. After a while the birds leave. The only sound left is the buzzing of insects. Anoo repeatedly moves his hand to keep one pesky fly from crawling on him. He looks closely at it and sees it's larger than a housefly and covered in fuzzy golden hairs brightly lit by a little patch of sun. He touches Laurel to get her attention. She looks at it until it flies away and says, "Beauty surrounds us. The blue sky with puffy white clouds. Patches of sun through the leaves lighting up the forest floor and shifting with the breeze. The call of birds and the buzzing of insects. The golden hair of a fly."

"Your face, your spirit, the two of us joined," adds Anoo.

"Beauty in things large and small," continues Laurel. "In a long life, in moments, in a grand vista, in the petals of a flower, in a long romance, in the intensity of sexual release. Was our joining everything you wanted it to be, Anoo?"

"Everything and more, Laurel. I want the beauty of this day together to grow into a lifetime."

"Thank you for that, Anoo. I want to nap next to you now."

After a nap and a light meal of dried fruit and pinyon nuts Laurel is thinking of a life together and children.

"Give me an example of how we would teach our kids to develop an independent perspective, Anoo."

"Okay, give me a second. Let's go back to who's smarter—men or women—and we'll say women are because they're always thinking."

"Okay, but first, what we said before was that the smartest individual is the one who finds the least amount of truth in coarse generalities like men are this or women are that," reminds Laurel.

"Yes, and so, an example using extremes would work to show the flaw in the 'women are smarter' perspective."

"An extreme example like—is a sixteen-year-old young woman really smarter than a seventy-year-old sharp-as-a-tack grandfather?" offers Laurel.

"And the answer is no. There is more to being smart than gender."

"Wouldn't it be smart to define smart?"

"Yes it would, Miss Smarty. Smart is learning about a subject. A person is smart about a subject or category of information based on how much they've learned on that particular subject. In this case the subject would be developing an independent perspective."

"And an independent perspective is what you're using to debunk the concept that women are smarter than men because women are always thinking, which is a coarse perspective as shown by using an extreme example. So, using extreme examples is one way to explain to a child where there is a flaw in perspective. Thus, showing them there is an opportunity for their own perspective to develop. Okay, go back to why the statement 'women are smarter than men because they're always thinking' is false," encourages Laurel.

"It's because the value system, the concept, and so the resultant conclusion are based on a false value system," states Anoo.

"The conclusion is that women are smarter than men. The proof of the concept is that women are always thinking. What is the flawed value system?" prompts Laurel.

"The flawed value system is that 'always thinking' is a quantity. The flaw, from my perspective, is that quality of thought is more important in being smart than quantity of thought. Quality of thought isn't considered in the concept that is being used to support the conclusion."

"We've already talked about how quality of thought is shown by a thought where 'the light goes on,'" Laurel remembers. "So, in some instances, we'd teach our children to have an independent perspective by using extreme examples and in other instances we'd have them check their value systems." And then she asks, "What's 'the light goes on'?"

"That's a tough one. I'll say it's known by the occurrence or the experience."

"That's not well thought out. I'll say it's the creation in the brain of a new synaptic connection. A new connection that in the future will be used in other patterns of thought and so will be used to organize concepts."

"What's 'other patterns of thought'?" asks Anoo.

"The patterns are in thoughts that contain or follow the same logical sequence or thoughts that are similar in nature."

"And those thoughts that are similar in nature can be organized into a concept. That's an impressive perspective, Laurel. I want to go back to your asking what's 'the light goes on.'"

"How so?"

"The light goes on is a spark. Enough sparks and you'll cause a fire. The mind is a fire waiting to be lit. We'll want to light the fires of our children's minds."

"I like that, Anoo. How else will we encourage our children to develop their own potential?"

"There's the idea of subtle oppression or subtle bias. We would want to make sure we are as encouraging towards a daughter's interest in math and science as a son's."

"The corollary for the son might be his interest in cooking or weaving," contributes Laurel.

"I have another area I'd like to include with this concept," continues Anoo.

"Okay, I'm ready."

"I think the oppression of the validity of a male's perceptive feelings is anything but subtle in many instances."

"I feel like I'm already in agreement but make your point," encourages Laurel.

"The accuracy of a male's perceptive feelings is considered substandard by females and that perspective is communicated early on in such a majority of male's lives that the male's capability itself is diminished."

"I feel like you're exposing a societal crime. I haven't thought of this before. Tell me more, Anoo."

"This diminishment of the accuracy of a male's perceptive feelings leads to an inability for males to communicate their feelings. I think it leads to an increase in head butting or pissing contest types of behavior. An increase in violent confrontations in interactions with others."

"I think there is a lot of truth in what you're saying. The idea is new to me. I need to let the idea sink in for your compelling argument to fully register with me. Can we take a break or change the subject?" asks Laurel.

"I want to change the subject. How will you teach our children to leave their bodies in a dream state?"

"That is a change in subject! Okay, I'll start with the idea that leaving one's body in a dream state is not unusual for people in general."

"That would mean the awareness of it happening is the stumbling block. How would you increase the awareness of the event?" asks Anoo.

"I would suggest the person lie comfortably flat on their back, with a small pillow under their head when they're not exhausted and therefore not in immediate need for sleep."

"And then what?" Anoo prompts.

"They focus the same attention towards their closed eyes as they would if they were looking out at something interesting."

"The same attention but with no stimuli. Would that create in the person a need for visual stimuli?"

"That's roughly what I'm thinking. It would be an effort to activate the visual receptors in the brain without input through the eyes."

"I see. Keep going."

"Well," continues Laurel, "then the person needs to be patient. When I focus my attention like that I'll start to feel like I want more. I'll want to do something, so I go do something."

"The first part, relax with awareness, sounds like meditation. I'll sit by the river, sometimes eyes closed sometimes open, and be aware of myself without the activity or stimulus of thoughts."

"I do that too, sometimes just because I like to," says Laurel. "Other times, if I'm feeling a little disrupted, out of sorts or not well physically I'll try to produce the effect of the physical vibrations of Om in myself. I'll try and move those vibrations around my body or over my entire body. Depending on the effect I want."

"The effect you want like to a particular place on your body if you're physically hurting or over your entire body if you're feeling emotionally disrupted," suggests Anoo.

"That's right. And vibrations that aren't as physical but are sort of all-encompassing are what I feel as I'm about to move out of my body in a dream state."

"You're a very interesting person, Laurel."

"Thank you, Anoo. If our children ask, 'If a tree falls in the forest and there is no one there to hear, does it make a sound?' you would say?"

"Of course it does. The earth has been around for some four billion years, trees for some two hundred million. The notion that something different will happen when they abruptly come together based on whether a person is around or not is extremely self-righteous," answers Anoo.

"That would show our children there is justification to the life around them without involving people," says Laurel. "Then you're not a proponent of idealism? The concept that the physical world is generated by people?"

"I've seen too many plants, animals, and minerals come and go with no influence from people to believe that. Plants and animals live their lives from birth to reproduction and ultimately death with no influence from people, all day, every day, in remote corners of the earth and in backyards. Inanimate objects turn into something new all the time without the benefit of people. Rocks erode into soil, and minerals recombine often through physical and chemical interactions with water. I think individuals can change their perspective of the world around them. I don't think the physical world changes when a person's perspective changes. I don't think the physical world is dependent on humanity for its existence," explains Anoo. After a reflective pause he asks, "And if our children ask you, my luscious Laurel, is the glass half full or half empty?"

"If the glass was full and someone drank half I'd say half emptied. If it was empty and then filled halfway I'd say half filled."

"And if you just walked in a room and didn't know how the glass got that way?"

"I'd say I don't know, I don't have enough information to base a conclusion on. Which would show our children it's okay to say, 'I don't know' when they need to learn more on a subject. And if they ask you, my amorous Anoo, which came first, the chicken or the egg?"

"I'd answer based on evolution. Something like a chicken but not quite a chicken laid the egg. This would teach them about the history of life on Earth. And if they ask, my lusting Laurel, where do babies come from?"

"I'd say, as far as I know, the stork brings them. Go ask your father what he thinks. Hey! Just because my breasts are poking up, looking for attention, doesn't mean you can pinch that hard."

"I'm so sorry. I better kiss them and make them better."

"That was too quick a kiss. I think the necessary apology would be a slow circling with your tongue and a light suck... Much better... and now the other please."

After some touching and feeling, rubbing and enjoying, giving and receiving, Anoo stops and looks at Laurel.

"What is it, Anoo? I can feel you're ready."

"Physically I am. But I'm really not."

"Tell me what you're feeling and thinking."

"I think I'm feeling too much like receiving my own pleasure and not enough like giving or sharing with you. Too much like I want to be physically inside you and not enough like I want to be deep inside your eyes, your heart."

"That sounds human, Anoo. We all have parts of ourselves that are self-centered and self-serving."

"I thought that would go away with you."

"I think it will with more time together and more sharing our bodies. Just a week ago we didn't have any idea this enormous change in our lives was going to happen. And we've all been hurt. Some of us have felt the abruptness of a quick departure or the lashing out of a vindictive person. We've all had the idyllic musings of youth succumb to the reality of two people's bodies and lives coming together. We've all indulged our needs in situations less than what we'd prefer."

"Thank you for that, Laurel. I think there's another part too."

"Tell me."

"I don't need to be inside you physically, now, because of our earlier couplings. I want to again, because I want to share with you. Somehow, sharing without the immediacy of lust has me feeling more naked."

"You're feeling vulnerable without the emotional defense of lust. I think that is very human," Laurel comforts. "I want us to be together, our bodies, our lives, our selves."

"That is what I want too. This has happened very quickly."

"I think that is all you're feeling. I won't ever try to wound you, Anoo. We may hurt each other. Two independent lives can't come together without some conflict. We will find ourselves in situations we will have to work out, situations that won't just fall into place. We'll do the best we can. We'll talk, give space, time for reflection, and time for emotions to calm. We'll come back together."

"I want to be together with you again, Laurel."

"Yes please."

"You have the most beautiful brown eyes."

"The blue of yours is lighter than the sky behind you."

"I like this feeling of being inside you as I look into your eyes. It feels like all of me is involved."

"I can feel you deep inside me. It's a feeling that reaches up to my heart and goes out to you."

"I can feel your heart feeding mine. Letting mine grow larger. That feeling grows up to my eyes and out to you," Anoo describes.

"I can feel my heart growing up to my eyes and out into yours too, my blue-eyed man."

"You put energy into me, my brown-eyed girl, that goes up to my heart then out into yours. From your heart to your eyes and then into mine. It's as though we're two circles of energy. From our joining parts to our hearts and from our hearts to our eyes."

"It's as though, we, are one circle of energy, encompassing two smaller, individual, circles of energy that each go in both directions. We're yin and yang, Anoo."

After a nap and some quiet time awake, Laurel begins to wonder what the next days will bring.

"What are we going to do tomorrow, Anoo?"

"We'll go to Mateen's later on in the afternoon and the next day to the farm."

"Where I'll prove my worth to you by getting up at first light, starting a fire, cooking everyone breakfast, and then working all day in the fields. At night, I cook and then clean half the night while everyone else sleeps?"

"If that's what you'd like. Otherwise you'll just fit into the routine where it works out best for you and everyone else."

"I think I like your version better. But first, what about tomorrow?"

"You mean at Mateen's?"

"I mean in the afternoon. I'd like us to go to camp so you can meet everyone, or whoever is around. Some of the shepherds will be away from camp. Grandfather will go with us to Mateen's. He'd like to stay there a few days and visit."

"I'm sure that's fine with Mateen. They've already talked about it. I'll mention it again tonight. And you're certainly right, I should meet the people at camp."

"Thanks for that. I want to keep talking but I need to move around a little."

"Okay, me too."

They both get up and stretch and walk around the little space between trees that they're in. After a few minutes of loosening up, Laurel asks, "Do you want to walk and talk?"

"I don't like to move far from my pack or walk around naked with a pack on."

"Let's stay naked and close by."

"I'd like that."

"Anoo?"

"Yes, Laurel?" responds Anoo wondering.

"Would you dance with me?"

"Dance?" asks Anoo, a little taken aback.

"Please dance with me, Anoo."

Laurel moves away from Anoo and dances back toward him. Anoo raises his arms to hold her but she twirls behind him and touches his hip with her hand and then runs her hand over his lower back to his other hip as she dances around him before dancing away again. She moves toward him doing a hula, moving her hips and arms to her own music. Anoo is a little mesmerized and unsure of what to do. She stops in front of him and raises his hands to her shoulders. Anoo understands and as she turns around in a circle he lets his hands run across her upper chest and then upper back as she turns. Facing away from him Laurel slowly dances away, her hips swaying and arms flowing out away from her and back in and then out to the other side. She turns and looks at him, hips moving, while her arms reach out toward him and then back to her chest. Anoo drinks in her beauty and her sensuous dance. He moves toward her feeling his feet in the grass, his knees flexing as his weight shifts from hip to hip. He raises his arms up above his head and then out to his sides palms up as he lifts his face to the sky. She turns, her back to him; he puts his hands under her hair. As she moves away her hair falls from his hands against her back. She keeps dancing away and turns, facing him again. Anoo dances toward her as she looks him up and down. He draws close to her and then raises his arms out to her. She does the same, their hands not quite touching. He half turns away from her and takes a half step, his foot tapping the ground, a full step with his other foot, and he stomps. A half step with one foot and a full step with the other, he turns a circle around her as she turns to keep facing him while dancing her slow hula. Tap and stomp he dances his heartbeat, da-dum da-dum da-dum. He raises his arms above his head and looks up past his hands to the green leaves and then to the blue sky. He brings his arms down and pushes them toward her. She catches his feeling and pushes it back to him. He keeps revolving around her as she rotates to face him. Her earth to his moon. Her sun to his earth. Her center to his circling dance. They dance until moments are eternities. The truth of their feelings for each other is seen and felt in every flowing movement. Moment to moment time passes. Anoo dances up to Laurel and she takes his hands and puts them on her shoulders. Turning in his arms she leans her moving body against his and pulls his hands to her breasts. He squeezes and hugs her close as she dances in his arms. A few minutes later Anoo dances her to the edge of the trees where they look out from their shaded sanctuary to the open bright meadow. Tomorrow they'll meet the other people in their lives. Today has been and is theirs.

After a few minutes they turn around and dance back into the trees. Anoo moves away and starts to dance around Laurel in a circle again.

"I'm going to dance up some energy to give you," he says.

"Dance up energy?"

Without responding Anoo continues dancing around Laurel. As he does, he raises his arms and fans his hands inward like he is pulling water in toward his chest. He holds his hands about a foot apart, one above the other. Right foot forward, left hand up. Left foot forward, right hand up. He moves his hands like they are circling around a ball in front of him. He concentrates on the space between his hands and feels tension grow. He pushes his hands closer together like he is compacting the ball. He relaxes his hands apart as he inhales and pushes them together as he exhales. Fingers don't touch but he feels something building between his hands. Tension builds between his hands. He turns to Laurel and steps in close to her. Without his fingers touching each other or touching Laurel he pushes his ball of energy into her solar plexus. She gasps and inhales. He goes back to his dance and builds another ball of energy. This time he moves around behind her and pushes his ball of energy into the base of her spine. She straightens and her face lifts to the sky. She tries this strange dance. She can feel something building between her hands. There is something there and she wants to give it to Anoo. She pushes it into him and his arms raise up and he looks to the sky. They look at each other and hug their pounding hearts together.

"How did you come up with that dance?" asks Laurel.

"I just started doing it when I felt too much energy to keep to myself. I got better with a little practice and developed a technique."

"Who do you give it to when I'm not with you?"

"Whatever is around me like flowers or trees, or old girlfriends from the very distant past," he adds, smiling. "Sometimes I store the energy in my medicine bag for later."

"Your medicine bag?" asks Laurel.

Anoo goes to his pile of clothes and takes the bag out from inside his shirt and shows it to her.

"I wondered if that was a medicine bag. I've felt it when we've hugged. What's in it?"

"It's supposed to be personal and private."

"Tell me anyway because you're you, I'm me, and we're together now."

"That's a convincing argument. There's an assortment of things. A water-smoothed stone to represent the cycle of water on this beautiful planet."

"Ocean to air, rains to the ground, and back to the air through the breath of plants. What else?"

"A snail fossil, that's for all life on Earth. Before people were, now, and when people are no more."

"Is there more?" asks Laurel.

"An elk's tooth. That's for all the lives I've taken to sustain mine."

"And?"

"A dried flower for all the beauty that surrounds us, that's all. I'm a little surprised you don't have one," says Anoo.

"I do—it's in my carry bag."

"And in it?"

"Is personal and private."

"Now, Laurel!"

"Okay, okay, but you'll think it's a little gross."

"I'm surprised to hear you say that but go on."

"Well, you told me what's in yours, so, there's the dried heart and lungs of a dove I killed and ate so its spirit would be inside me. That's for the peace and love I want to feel in my beating heart with every breath I take."

"Interesting, and?"

"There's some soil from our garden that plants reach their roots down in to, grow up towards the sun from, and turn into food for us."

"I like that. Is there more?"

"Yes, some of Grandfather's hair. That's for family lineage."

"Respectful. And?"

"A hawk talon."

"For the soaring freedom of your spirit."

"Actually, one of my mother figures gave it to me to commemorate my first cycle of becoming a woman. She said my name reflects the softness and beauty I will have as a woman; the talon is so my perspective as a woman will be as sharp as a hawk's sight."

"I'm very impressed. You certainly took a different tack than I did. But medicine bags are intended to be individual."

"After that sharing, Anoo, I want us to share our bodies again."

They explore how their bodies cause the other to feel, and then they walk back to their meeting place.

"I thank you, my lovely Laurel, for a day like no other I've ever had. I couldn't have imagined this day being better. I want us together every day."

"Thank you for saying so, Anoo. I want our lives to be shared. The sharing of two individuals in a passionate love."

"I love you, Laurel."

"I love you, Anoo."

Chapter Seven

AFTER THE PLEASURE of a hug and a kiss and looking into each other's eyes and another hug and a kiss:

"Good morning, Laurel."

"Good morning to you, Anoo."

"Did you have a nice night?"

"Yes, after I was questioned by my girlfriends."

"Questioned?"

"They wanted to know how our joining day was. I let them know it was more than I could have hoped. That explanation, however, just piqued their interest. Had the circumstances been reversed I would have been asking the questions, so I didn't mind. Did you and Mateen talk?"

"Just small talk. I went to sleep soon after dinner."

"And what should we do today, my handsome man?"

"How about a walk and a talk and indulging in naked pleasures."

"We do think alike."

"I guess we only have about half the day."

"Should I get naked right now?" asks Laurel, laughing.

"I was thinking we just shouldn't walk very far, but okay."

"I guess we should walk first," says Laurel, smiling.

After finding an older aspen stand with large trees and grasses cured by the summer's heat the loving couple settles in.

"Tell me about the farm. Sleeping, bathing, working, give me a little introduction. Who else might I meet?"

"For sleeping there's my room or the loft in the barn if we'd like a little more privacy. I guess if our sleeping together is too big a change I could sleep in the barn and you in my room."

"Let's go with sleeping together at first. And maybe the loft at first. What's that like?"

"In the fall it's very nice. Not many bugs as it has cooled down. I sleep out there often enough just for a change. Sometimes I sleep there because of one critter or another raiding the crops and it's easier for me to get up and take the dogs out to roust them from there. We'll have water up there and a pee pot. There's stairs going to the loft the dogs and cats use. They'll want to snuggle in with us."

"I like the sound of that. Let's sleep in the loft. What about bathing?"

"I usually swim twice a day in the summer. In the morning and then in the afternoon after working. As it cools in the fall I only go in the afternoon. There's a shower in the house that we can heat up. That's more of a cold weather thing though. We can sweat lodge by the river and jump in after, that's always nice. In the winter we fire up the sauna and hot tub room next to the barn."

"Hot tub room? What's that like?"

"It's a pretty small, low-roofed room that heats up quick. There's a stove we heat water and rocks on. The floor is graveled, so there's no concern for where the water goes. There's a shower for washing up and the tub for indulgent soaking. There's also a couple chairs and a platform to rest on while pouring water on hot rocks for steam."

"That sounds wonderful. We have enough water concerns that we can't have a hot tub. The steamy sweat lodge is what we do. Town has hot tub rooms like you describe. They have the river right nearby for their water. How about working?"

"There's lots to do. Mateen will be down a few weeks after us. He always helps with the harvest. We do work pretty much all day but there's always time for a break to swim or stretch. There's no reason to strain yourself. Even when things are ripening quickly in the fall everything doesn't ripen in the same few days. Last year we did have to get the neighbors to help us harvest the apples. Most years they can stay on the trees until after a few frosts so there's no real hurry. Last year a big flock of grackles focused on them and wouldn't leave. We had to pick them quickly before they all ended up with peck holes."

"What did you do then, after having to pick them all at once?"

"They last in the root cellar for a quite a while. What we couldn't fit in there was still okay for a while in the coolest shade like the north side of the barn. It was mostly getting them off the trees that was the hurry."

"Who does what? Harvesting, cleaning, and preparing?"

"Everyone does everything. Generally, we're harvesting in the morning then cleaning and storing later."

"What's involved with storing?"

"It depends on what we've harvested. We dry, can, and some types of veggies can just be moved into the root cellar."

"Can the stuff drying stay out all night?"

"Probably not, even with us sleeping in the barn. We'll move stuff into the barn so we can keep an eye on things at night. Mateen can sleep in my room. That will work out well. What else are you wondering?"

"Will we go to town and meet your friends? Will anyone come out to the farm?"

"My aunt Cassie and her boyfriend will come out. They'll want to meet you and they always come out and work during harvest anyway. Our nearest neighbors will want to meet you too. We usually get together every month or so with them for an evening meal, so no real pressure on you. We can think about going to town. See what we want to do."

"I might be a little overwhelmed as it is."

"That would be fine. We'll see. What else would you like to talk about?" asks Anoo.

"I want our bodies to have a deep conversation with each other."

"That was a very nice conversation, my lovely Laurel."

"It was my pleasure, Anoo."

"What other topic would you like to talk about?"

"How about nature versus nurture," suggests Laurel.

"That sounds interesting, you start."

"First, I don't think nature versus nurture is well put."

"How so?" asks Anoo.

"I think it should be nature versus learned versus intended."

"So, nature is what we start with or have biologically. Learned is what we're exposed to, and then there's what we intend. Please go on."

"Who is the real person, so to speak?" asks Laurel. "I think I could use any societal division to make my point, for example, religious, national, or racial."

"I'm following, keep going."

"I don't think any of those divisions are from nature. I think they're all learned. A person can be taught racial bias from an early age. They can then learn to change their perspective but not quite be able to shake off their early exposure. Who, then, is the person? Are they their early exposure or their later learning and intent to change, even if that intent to change isn't one hundred percent effective?"

"I'll go with what they intend, who they try to be," says Anoo.

"If the person considers their heart to be a true statement of their self they would be who their early exposure caused them to be."

"Because they couldn't change their early exposure totally. Keep going," Anoo encourages.

"That's right and, also, not fair to the individual. The heart would be where the bias is. The bias wouldn't be caused by the individual's nature or intent but their early exposure. I'm using heart as behavior learned too early on for the young child to resist. Causing a bias that wouldn't be able to be totally changed by intent. Intent being used by the individual to cause learned behavior."

"Okay, then during that process of individually causing one's own learned behavior the person will feel like they're making an effort," adds Anoo. "Like they're working against their heart. They would also know they're working toward a goal they believe is right. A goal they believe to be a more accurate statement of their individual perspective."

"That's what I'm saying," agrees Laurel. "That discomfort of relearning isn't a statement of error in what the individual is trying to learn. It's a statement of the error in what the individual was taught at an early age. Early learning is done on a blank slate. At an early age, there's nothing to compare to, nothing to cause discomfort as one is taught."

"So, nature doesn't have inherent bias; it's taught, and so becomes heartfelt. Trying to change that early teaching causes the individual to feel as though they're working against their true self. After some work, however, that process can result in a more accurate and comprehensive perspective," concludes Anoo.

"Yes, and I think the same thinking goes along with the idea that perceptive feelings aren't inherently accurate."

"How so?"

"Perceptive feelings are based on one's value systems, experiences, beliefs, and become heartfelt with repeated use. That heartfelt feeling of truth can change if a new piece of information is learned."

"Often learned by communication with the person that the perceptive feeling is being directed toward," adds Anoo.

"That's right, and that's when perceptive feelings are the most accurate, after learning of individual situations or perspectives."

"So then, perceptive feelings don't come from a godlike truth. What they are based on is learned, and that learning can be, and should be, changing as one gains information and perspective in life."

"I love talking to you, Anoo. Learning and changing can cause some discomfort but it is necessary for individual growth and to root out early biases."

"That is a really impressive perspective and very well communicated. What would you like to do now, my lovely, curvy, naked Laurel?"

130

"We could talk some more," she suggests, laughing.

"Sure, we can talk while we're joined," says Anoo, laughing too.

"Okay, I'm ready."

"Well, I'm wanting to but not quite ready."

"Lie down, my strong, handsome man. I'll give you a hand and then I'm going to put you in an advantageous position for me."

After a few minutes Anoo says, "Your advantage is my pleasure."

"When I introduce you at camp will I be telling everyone we're a couple and that after harvest we'll be living together at winter camp?"

"Being a coupling couple with you is better than I could have imagined, Laurel. What I can't imagine is spending the winter without you."

"Can I tell everyone we're a loving couple, not just two people who love to couple with each other?"

"I love you, Laurel. I want to share my life with you."

"I love you too, Anoo."

After a very enjoyable joining Laurel says, "Let's really take a walk, Anoo. Then we'll need to go to camp."

"A walk on this beautiful day with my beautiful woman. Can I say you're mine? I have, like 'my lovely Laurel.' Now I'm wondering if I should."

"You're my man, I'm your woman. You're in my life, I'm in yours. It's an equal statement of fact, not a statement of dominance."

"That will work. Where are we headed?"

"Let's just wander around but basically towards camp."

It's a beautiful day for young lovers. The air is hot but there's a breeze and enough clouds to make walking in sunny meadows and shady tree stands equally nice. The clouds show the possibility of a late afternoon or early evening thunderstorm. As they near camp they meet up with Laurel's friends who have wandered a little in anticipation of meeting the man who has become so important in their friend's life.

"Hi, Anoo!" Briana calls out enthusiastically.

"Hey, Anoo! It's nice to finally meet you. We've heard about you every night since you guys met," says Teresa.

"Hi to you both."

"Anoo, this is Briana and Teresa. My very good and very inquisitive friends."

"It's nice to meet you, Briana, and you, Teresa. I'm sure your inquisitiveness is out of concern for Laurel and not just looking for gossip."

"Anoo, did you have as nice a joining day yesterday as our Laurel did?"

"Briana!"

"Okay, I might have been wrong about the gossiping part," admits Anoo.

"It looks to me like he did. And, Laurel, you're glowing!" notices Teresa.

"I think Anoo looks a little tired. Have you been pushing Laurel around all day?"

"Briana!"

"My apologies, Anoo. It's very nice to meet you," Briana says while curtsying and laughing.

"Yes, it's nice to meet you, Anoo," says Teresa, offering her hand to him before throwing her arms around him in a big hug.

"My turn, my turn," says Briana.

"I do have to admit, Anoo, that you've been the most news we've had in camp all summer," explains Laurel.

"Maybe all the summers. We're glad you two look like a happy couple."

"You'll have to excuse Briana. She finds the wide-open spaces of camp more confining, in a way, than a tavern," explains Laurel.

"Speaking of socializing in a tavern, do you have any single friends, Anoo?" asks Teresa.

"Oh, you two! Come on, Anoo, let's meet Grandfather," says

Laurel, taking his hand and as they turn, "I love them both dearly and if either of them brought a man to camp I'd be doing the same."

"I actually do know a couple guys who'd like to meet girls as attractive as you two," says Anoo over his shoulder.

"No wonder Laurel likes him so much; he really sees people for who they are," says Briana, laughing.

"Where does she think she's going?" asks Teresa from two steps behind Laurel and loud enough to hear. "Some place we're not going to follow?"

"Still, I must apologize for these two," continues Laurel, ignoring Teresa.

"I like them both already," says Anoo.

"Please don't encourage them," says Laurel. "It's like throwing a ball for a retriever. Anoo, this is my grandfather. You can call him Grandfather."

"Hello, Anoo. It's nice to meet you."

"Hello, Grandfather. It's nice to meet you too. I want to thank you for giving Laurel and me a chance to meet. The last few days have been some of the best of my life."

"I'm glad for you both, Anoo. I like the excitement for the future I see in Laurel since you've met. I understand you're taking her to your farm for harvest."

"I am, and then we're planning on going to your winter camp. If that's all right with you."

"You are most certainly welcome."

"Thank you, Grandfather. I understand you'll accompany us to the cabin."

"I'm looking forward to a visit with my old friend Mateen."

"We're going too!" explains Briana.

"No, you're not. This is still my and Anoo's time. Oh, like sticking your tongue out at me is going to change my mind."

"We're at least walking with you to where you guys met. We haven't even been able to go there yet because Laurel didn't want us to interfere," says Teresa. "She seems to think we'd be intrusive."

"You mean she didn't want the competition," says Briana and then to Laurel, "And you sticking out your tongue doesn't impress me either."

"Why don't we sit? I'm sure some of the others would like to say hello," says Grandfather.

Anoo meets everyone staying at camp except the shepherds who are out with the herd. This is unavoidable, but too bad. Some of them will be the ones left in camp when Laurel and Anoo get back after they help with the harvest. After a nice visit Laurel says good-bye to everyone in camp because she'll be gone for a couple of months. Briana and Teresa walk to the couple's meeting place before saying their good-byes. The walk to the cabin is pleasant. They find Mateen waiting on the porch for them.

"Hello, my old friend, and welcome to my home."

"It's nice to see you again, Mateen. I'd like you to meet my grand-daughter Laurel."

"It's a pleasure to see you again, Laurel. Our next meeting will be in a few weeks, not twenty years."

"Grandfather says we've met. For me of course this seems like the first time. I'm honored to meet you and thank you for bringing Anoo and me together."

"We both gave you two an opportunity. What you've done with that opportunity is yours and it pleases us."

"Thank you and may I hug you?"

"Yes please. And I'd like to invite you all inside."

After some small talk and catching up with Grandfather, Mateen moves some chairs around in the main room of his cabin. There are some peals of thunder in the distance with gusty winds and spits of rain. It won't last long but the smell of water on sagebrush and dried grass permeates the air. Mateen and Grandfather sit next to each other facing Anoo and Laurel. Anoo and Laurel sit with their shoulders touching and holding each other's hand. The two kind, wise men of many years communicate with their hearts and through their minds to the hearts and minds of the young couple before them. The men take turns but communicate as one.

You are both good people. We are proud of who you've made yourselves into. Your bodies are strong. Your minds bright. Your spirits are a light you are now sharing. Your sharing a goodness equally to each. We want to say to you things we've said before. Things for you to remember as you live your lives together.

Correctness, accuracy, truth is to be based on the content of what is said. Not on who is talking. Do not mistake the ability to walk forward under the weight of the yoke of tyranny and authoritarianism as freedom. Hierarchies are for those who need other people's structures. There is no hierarchy, not religious, societal, governmental, or intellectual that you as individuals cannot reach beyond. Define your own value systems. Start with the golden rule. Don't do violence; legitimate defense is not violence. Don't be angry; be tolerant. Don't be selfish or greedy; be compassionate. Don't be self-centered; be considerate. Truth is in the eye of the beholder. Your truth is based on your value systems, your experiences, your choices. Be clear, be direct, be aware. As you increase awareness of who you are, what lives in your subconscious will diminish. As you define yourselves, vagueness will decrease. Losing vagueness will be accompanied by a decrease in deceit, manipulation, greed, and other self-centered behaviors as assuredly as your hearts are good.

Do not be concerned that an increase in awareness will decrease the magic in your lives. The magic of coincidence and timing. The magic of bringing toward yourselves unexpected encounters with unexpected consequences. The magic of bringing yourselves toward wonders you couldn't have sensed through your normal senses. Increasing awareness and clarity will only decrease the appearance of magic as it is seen through superstition and vagueness. Increasing awareness will allow you to define the edges of the places where magic is found, for that magic we speak of is a real thing. The magic of timing, coincidence, and unexpected value. That magic won't go away with awareness. Awareness of that magic will cause it to become recognizable and repeatable. Increasing awareness of yourselves will increase the desire to be tolerant of others, increase compassion for others. Choose to help each other in your daily lives. Share your thoughts, feelings, and bodies openly with each other. Grow as individuals so you can have more to share with each other, more to bring together into one couple. Feel the breeze on your sweaty, tired bodies, the cool moisture of dew on your bare feet, the heat of the sun on your skin. See the colors of the sunset in the petals of flowers. Hear the light trill of the flute in the songs of birds. Feel the beat of the drum as your feet push up from the ground in the dance of life. Plant seeds and watch them grow through a season. Plant trees and watch them grow over years. Have thoughts like a bee feeding from flowers, purposely move from here to there, sample, linger where you want. Have the perspective of a soaring hawk, the concerned awareness of its prey. Perceive your life through the lifetime of a tree, through the midge's brief, but complete, span of life. Swim through water, run through air, jump into the sky, fall down, and get up, live life. It is the most wondrous experiment imaginable. Push yourself and each other. Reach out your hand, your heart, your thoughts. Shelter in a chrysalis when you must. Spread your wings when you can. Speak in poetry. Laugh at yourself and with each other. Embrace the gift of your time here on this beautiful earth, your time here, now, together. Peace to you both.

After some time to absorb what has been said and how it was said Laurel warmly says,

"Thank you, Grandfather, thank you, Mateen. For your words and for this experience."

"Thank you both. And what can we do for you now?" Anoo asks.

"Make us some dinner!" replies Grandfather.

"And bring us a drink!" adds Mateen.

This, Laurel and Anoo do with reverent enjoyment for these wonderful men in their lives. As their soup simmers and biscuits bake Laurel brings Grandfather Anoo's new flute and Mateen taps out a lively rhythm on one of his drums. Their young friends dance around the cabin. The soup ready, they all move out to the back porch for dinner and quiet conversation. The clouds are passing, the stars will be out soon. After eating, the young couple clean up the kitchen as they enjoy listening to the music coming from the porch. They go out and dance slowly in each other's arms to soft music as Mateen sings songs using lyrical syllables with feeling, instead of words. As the sky becomes dark the young couple walk around to the front of the cabin and out into the aspen stand. Laurel lies down in the tall grass on her long skirt. Looking up at the stars coming out she pulls up the front of her skirt. As Anoo stirs up the pot of her loving goodness she dances all around him. They couple until their hearts join and their eyes meet and they each become together.

Chapter Eight

AFTER A REFRESHING night's sleep everyone is up early. Laurel and Anoo enjoy listening to Grandfather and Mateen reminisce as they eat breakfast and prepare for their walk to the farm. After filling up and cleaning up they all sit facing each other again.

"Where do you want to end up?" asks Mateen.

"You want to be the process, not the result," answers Grandfather.

"You start with not knowing," continues Mateen. "The ultimate vagueness. Then you learn. You learn a language, family patterns, societal customs, religious basics, the character and personalities of people close to you."

"You learn the first base you interpret the world from," says Grandfather succinctly.

"A base created from nothing," explains Mateen. "Refined over years, until that base can be used to interpret the events occurring around you through perceptive feelings. An interpretation that comes to the person out of their subconscious to a feeling."

"That base feels like truth, your true self," Grandfather elaborates. "Like something greater than you because it seems to be coming from some place other than you. It is not greater than you, it *is* you. It is where you have accumulated your learnings, where you reply to yourself from. That base feels like truth for everyone. It feels like truth for people raised under different religions, in different societies, with different languages."

"That base is a good start," continues Mateen. "The process you've created as a child, primarily through adoption from parental figures, is a good process. Becoming more aware of your base and the process that creates it is also a good thing. That process can appear to be reaching out to something greater than you, a supreme being. That 'greater than you' is actually human consciousness that surrounds us all and that we are all a part of. When an individual taps into that human consciousness they are commonly tapping into the average of what is out there. They usually are not getting the arcane perspective of the most knowledgeable individual on a particular subject. That source of information, that human consciousness, is a reasonable place to start learning from. You can do better than the average on many subjects, not all but many. Grow your base by increasing perspective, by learning, changing, and growing. Grow your awareness of the process you use to interpret the world around you by intentionally determining the value systems you use in the process."

"Choosing opposites does not increase perspective," says Grandfather. "Increase perspective by learning and communicating and then apply that new learning to the process that results in a perceptive feeling. Large changes in perspective caused by learning something new will cause the process to feel uncomfortable, like you are no longer true to yourself. This discomfort is temporary and a part of learning. The discomfort doesn't show when merely learning a new piece of information. It comes from learning something that changes the value systems your perceptive feelings are based on. That temporary discomfort is a part of growing as a person."

"Intentionally changing the value systems your perceptive feelings are based on increases awareness of yourself, increases responsibility for yourself, increases your ability to grow," Mateen says with assurance based on experience. "After some time, parts of the process you have now intentionally created for yourself will go back into your subconscious. This is to speed up the process, not to go back to a lack of awareness of the process. Your base will, once again, feel like truth to you. Your discomfort, caused by intentionally changing your base, will pass."

"Until you learn something else new that will change your perspective enough to cause you to change your value systems again." Grandfather continues the thought. "This learning, changing, growing can and should continue your entire life. Keep your mind openly receptive to new thinking and it will. Be patient when you feel discomfort from intentionally changing the value systems you use to interpret the world around you. In time, you will learn to identify yourself with the process of changing your value systems. Not with what you've learned or how you reactively feel about someone or something."

"Identifying yourself with the process of changing your value systems will speed up your ability to learn and change and so grow," Mateen says. "Awareness of this process will decrease what you had perceived as coming from a supreme being. It will decrease the seeming randomness of the world around you. God doesn't work in mysterious ways. The individual works in mysterious ways when the individual is not aware of themselves. God doesn't act on humanity through violent nature. We live on a planet that is turbulent sometimes. God does not hinder us. We get in our own way when we leave our way in life to chance."

"How does one change the value systems used to interpret perceptive feelings?" asks Grandfather. "Start with being aware of the value systems you are currently using."

"Do you think God created the universe with life only on Earth?" asks Mateen. "Evolution and the perspective of a God that has seen many thousands of species of intelligent life come and go will take away the self-righteousness creationism fosters. Do you think that we are actors in a play God has already written? Choose to change that victim of circumstance perspective for the choice to create your own individuality. Take responsibility for yourself. Do you see others through generalities? A person is a man or a woman, so you then decide you know half that individual's character as quickly as you learn their name. An individual finds truth in a religion that you're familiar with, so then they must respond to a statement from you in a way you've come to expect. An individual is of a particular race, so you decide you know how they will act before they act. Take away that source of bias, of prejudice, by choosing to see others as individuals. Learn about their knowledge on a particular subject, what they yearn for, what has hurt them. Seeing another person as an individual reinforces the perspective that we are more alike than inherently different. It causes a desire to apply the golden rule to that individual. Do you think that truth, accuracy, being correct is based on who is talking? Change your perspective to where being correct is based on communicable information. Raise yourself and others above 'don't think— obey.'"

"People hold many value systems," Grandfather says in conclusion. "The ones we start with are not necessarily the ones we should keep throughout our lives. As we learn and change and grow as individuals our value systems should too. Your individual lives are an enormous opportunity. Explore, wonder, and test with awareness. Don't be a victim who reacts to life; choose to create yourself."

Grandfather and Mateen walk with Laurel and Anoo for two or three miles on the young couple's walk to the farm. They take their time, with Mateen pointing out interesting plants and talking about various sights he's seen around his cabin. After saying good-bye Mateen and Grandfather head back to the cabin for a few days of visiting. When they get back to the cabin Mateen lets Eli know the couple are on their way and gives an estimate on their arrival time. Laurel and Anoo make good time without rushing. They have about eighteen miles to go to the farm from where they said good-bye to Mateen and Grandfather. They slip through town without being noticed by any of Anoo's friends, which would delay their arrival at the farm. As they near the farm the dogs bark and the horses neigh sensing Anoo drawing near. Anoo greets his father with a hug and turns to introduce Laurel. He sees she's already being wrapped up in a hug from his mother, who's saying, "Hello, Laurel. I hope you don't mind a big hug. I get all the broad shoulder hard-chested hugs I want. A good boob-smooshing hug is nice variety for me."

"I don't mind, Tohlee?"

"Yes, please, call me Tohlee and this is Eli."

"Hello, Laurel. Welcome to our home."

"Thank you both for welcoming me so warmly. Thank you for the opportunity to help your family harvest your growing season of work and for me to be able to see where Anoo grew up."

"You are very welcome here. Your company will be our pleasure. Now, let's let the guys walk around the farm so Anoo can see what's been going on here and say hello to the animals."

As the guys walk away Tohlee asks:

"Would you like to see the house and my growing beds?"

"Yes, I would. Anoo has told me you grow a variety of herbs, spices, and medicinal plants. He even offered, when we first met, to race back here to bring me some seeds of plants we don't have."

"We'll make sure you're stocked up before you go to your winter camp. That would have been quite an effort for him to make."

"I decided that, as nice an offer as it was, I would rather spend that time getting to know him."

"You've had some days together and you're here. I know it hasn't been that long but are you a couple?"

"I cannot believe how much and enjoyably my life has changed in these last few days. I'm very much taken by your son and want to share many more days with him."

"To the degree that you and Anoo decide, you are welcome in our family. Consider me your friend. I'm looking forward to getting to know you."

"Thank you for such a warm welcome and your offer of friendship. I can see why Anoo has grown to be such a good-hearted man."

"You are most welcome. Come on in, stay in Anoo's room tonight. Settle in and then I'll show you what I grow."

—⦵—

"She's a very attractive woman, Anoo. I'll be direct. Has that influenced how rapidly you two seem to have progressed towards being a couple?" asks Eli.

"I absolutely think so. But I don't think unduly. I'd like to think that her beauty is more a statement of fact than a factor in becoming a couple."

"Well answered, my son. I'm sure I'll enjoy getting to know her and watching you two grow as a couple while you're here. Now take a look at these taters."

"That's a lot of wilt but not all that early." Then, looking closer. "What are these little jumpers?"

"Flea beetles."

"Do you think they've hurt the yield?" asks Anoo.

"Probably some. Like you said it's not all that early for them to die back but it is early. I first noticed the problem as little pin holes when you were here. I thought the plants could fight through them, so I didn't mention it; the holes were so small and there weren't that many. Then the numbers of holes grew as the population of beetles did and the holes got bigger as the beetles did."

"We can't sic the dogs on the little things. What are we going to do?"

"What about an early harvest? We won't let them sit in the ground like most years. Then we will burn what's left of the foliage and we won't plant anything in this section next year," suggests Eli.

"Can we mark the locations of the plants, pull and burn the foliage, then dig the taters later like we usually do? We'd still skip a year like you're saying and the next year plant something the beetles don't prefer. Or, will they live in the ground without the foliage?"

"I'm not sure. You can check with your aunt Cassie in town. The library may have something on them. I think pulling the foliage and burning it needs to happen right away though."

"Laurel and I can start on that tomorrow. We will use a wheelbarrow of small stones from the river to mark the plants and then gather and burn the foliage. Where do the things winter? Are they adults or eggs while they winter?" Anoo asks, not expecting an answer.

"I've dug a few plants up and haven't seen any damage to the taters themselves, just the foliage, so I think that plan will work for now. That's the biggest problem that's developed since you've been gone."

"How does the corn look?" asks Anoo.

"The sweet looks and tastes great. The flour and feed are both looking good too."

"Oh! I want some sweet for dinner, first of the season for me. I wonder if Laurel has ever had any right off the stalk? She's usually up at summer camp when it ripens."

"She's in for a treat if she hasn't. Let's go see what the girls are up to."

When they get back to the house the girls are walking around Tohlee's growing beds. Anoo goes inside to get hard cider for everyone as Eli arranges chairs on the east-facing porch. It's still early enough in the evening to be uncomfortable in the direct lowering sun on the west side.

"It's so beautiful here. I love the contrast between the order of your fields and the wild lands reaching to the horizon. The cottonwoods along the river are a border but also bring the two extremes together," remarks Laurel.

"I like that observation, Laurel. We've been very content here, haven't we, Eli?" asks Tohlee.

Eli doesn't respond immediately; he seems mesmerized by the scene.

"Perhaps he's not as content as I thought," says Tohlee, laughing.

"Sorry, Mateen and Grandfather wanted to engage me in their discussion about people's drive to spend humanity's future on war. I respectfully declined. They are glad you two are here relaxing with us. And I am very content to be here with you, my loving wife," responds Eli belatedly.

"I should probably challenge Grandfather more often along philosophical lines," says Laurel.

"Philosophizing definitely has its moments but not all the time," says Tohlee.

"Everything in moderation including moderation," adds Eli.

"I bet you could engage Grandfather in a way that would be enjoyable for him," Anoo encourages.

"I think I'll try harder; maybe I can be a good challenge for him," considers Laurel.

"And learn in the process," says Tohlee.

"I'm sure Mateen would appreciate a good challenge too," says Eli.

"Eli, do you want to join in their conversation?" asks Tohlee.

"It would be interesting. Think of those two with a lifetime of experience each. Debating and verbally parrying," says Eli.

"They teach by proving their points," says Anoo.

"With patience and clarity," says Laurel.

"They are good men. We do and should appreciate them for their perspective," says Tohlee.

"It's nice here, Anoo. I'm already becoming comfortable. Tohlee, Anoo said you moved here before he was born."

"I became pregnant about nine years after we moved from town."

"Establishing a farm, raising a son, you've done a lot of work here."

"Thank you. We had help from Mateen and my sister Cassie. Anoo has been a big help since he was quite young."

"Will I be meeting Cassie?"

"She'll be here in a few days. She's very happy for you, Anoo."

"I always look forward to her visits," says Anoo.

After some time appreciating the view and small talk Tohlee suggests, "Let's have some dinner and watch the sunset."

"I'll move the chairs to the west porch," says Eli.

"Can I help you, Tohlee?" asks Laurel.

"Let me show you the facilities and water, Laurel," says Anoo.

"I don't need any help, Laurel. Wander around a few minutes with Anoo."

After eating, everyone enjoys the sunset. There are enough scattered clouds to nicely color the sky. When one cloud bottom fades another lights up.

"What first attracted you to Anoo, Laurel?" asks Tohlee.

"He's very strong and handsome," replies Laurel.

"From little acorns mighty oaks grow," says Eli.

"He's intelligent and perceptive," continues Laurel.

"The apple doesn't fall far from the tree," says Eli with a smile.

"He's really adapting to me as I am to him. We're a very large change in each other's life."

"Like the willow they can bend," says Eli, laughing.

"And what attracted you to Laurel, Anoo?" asks Tohlee, smiling.

"She's sweet and beautiful but I wouldn't want to push her too far."

"A locust tree in flower. Perfumes the very air around her, attracts with her flowering beauty, but watch out for those thorns," says Eli barely able to contain himself.

"You'll have to excuse Eli; sometimes his momentum exceeds his sensibility," says Tohlee.

"I'm very much enjoying this banter, plus, I'm thinking I should exceed my sensibility more often," replies Laurel.

"Everything in moderation including not being moderate," says Eli.

"Now you're just repeating yourself. You used that concept before we ate. Well, you were more defined this time," admits Tohlee.

"Concepts repeat themselves—that's what makes them concepts. They're applicable to more than one situation," says Eli.

"We should be like concepts that apply to more than one situation. We should learn to adapt to new situations. It broadens our perspective," says Laurel.

"It's easier to adapt by being inclusive with our perspectives than to fight change," says Tohlee.

"Change is an opportunity to learn and grow," says Laurel.

"You know, Anoo, I like your new woman," says Tohlee. "She's intelligent, friendly, and courteous."

"She really is a pleasure to share our evening with, not to mention positive and perceptive," says Eli. "I'm glad she's here."

"I hope she doesn't mind our talking about her as though she isn't here," says Anoo, laughing.

"That's okay. I'm just a warm fuzzy ball right now."

"How big a ball?" asks Eli.

"A hundred giants couldn't wrap their arms around me like you all are doing right now."

"Yeah, I like her too," says Eli.

"I'm melting, but it's the opposite of water to a witch; with you guys I become more as I melt."

"Now I like her even more," says Eli.

As the sunset colors dim, Eli and Anoo walk the fields and orchard with the dogs. The farm animals are secure and nothing is raiding the crops. It's been an eventful day and work starts early on the farm. With good nights and see you in the morning, everyone retires.

"Is everything okay, Laurel?"

"I couldn't feel better about coming here with you, Anoo. Your parents are warm and welcoming people. Will it be hard for you to leave here for the winter?"

"Leaving here will be a change. Leaving here will continue our adventure together."

"We've never slept in a bed together, Anoo. Will you cover me up with the warmth of your body?"

Up early and then a hard day's work. Crops have been picked and stored. Flea beetles burned, hopefully never to return. Now, a familiar walk for Anoo. He remembers the last time he walked this path to his swimming hole and looked out from behind this willow. That was a week ago and everything has changed in his life. This time there are a woman's arms wrapped around his chest. A beautiful woman that he likes to talk to and be with is looking over his shoulder sharing this scene with him. A push from behind and they're out onto the gravel bar. Clothes off and they're wading out into the river. Anoo has been missing this and dives in. He swims out and turns around. Laurel is still standing waist deep.

"I'm not a good swimmer. I haven't had many opportunities."

"I'm sorry, I didn't think of that. Can you swim at all?"

"I just dog paddle and even that I haven't done very often in water this big."

"Paddle out to me and then we'll turn around and go back to where we can stand."

Standing chest deep Anoo loses his train of thought as he watches Laurel's breasts bobbing at water level.

"Anoo! Teach me to swim."

"Okay, okay, I just really like that effect. Let's go out to where it's just over your head and we'll tread water."

"How do I do that?"

"Kick with your feet and move your hands in little figure eights like this."

"I'm not going to know what to do with my feet."

"I'll go out to where I can barely stand and then you'll go out deeper with me holding your hands. Kick until you feel like you're pushing yourself up. Then I'll let go of one hand and you start doing the figure eights. I'll let go of your other hand if you're comfortable."

After some practice Laurel can tread water well enough to keep her head above water and they go back to the shallows.

"That's not really swimming."

"No, but it's what to do if you're having trouble. Get your head out of the water, breathe, and assess your situation."

"Okay, what's next?"

"Lay out flat. I'll hold you up with my arms under your belly. You'll practice kicking and some arm movements."

After some practice Laurel goes to shore and Anoo swims out to his favorite rock. Before going under he tells her what he's going to do so she won't worry. Back on shore he sits behind her and wraps his arms around her.

"You did really well, Laurel."

"How long can you stay under?"

"I usually stay under for a minute or so."

"Can you see fish?"

"Sometimes."

"I'm going to get good at this and then brag to the girls."

"I go every day, usually twice a day until it's too cold. You'll get plenty of practice."

"I'm not cold with your arms around me."

"You feel nice, slippery when wet."

Turning around and pushing Anoo onto his back.

"I want to slip down onto you."

After indulging in their ability to pleasure each other the young couple walk back to the farm.

"Hey, you guys."

"Hey, Tohlee. What's Eli up to?" asks Laurel, hearing a banging from the barn.

"He's putting up shelves for you. Anoo said you guys want to stay in the barn. You can be our guards. We hung a blanket up there for a privacy wall. The dogs and cats will want to stay with you, so we made them a bed up there too."

"Thank you."

"Come on, Laurel, I want to show you around my sewing room in more detail. Anoo, the harvest that's drying needs to be brought in."

"Okay."

After some end of the day chores and some girl bonding time the farmers find themselves watching another sunset after a well-earned dinner.

"What do you think, Laurel, could you adjust to the routine of farm work?" asks Eli.

"It seems like very good and rewarding work with some time for relaxing, like going swimming."

"Laurel is going to be an excellent swimmer in no time."

"You're a good teacher."

"You can't swim?" asks Eli.

"Not well yet. I haven't been many times."

"Your friends Briana and Teresa, what are they doing this evening?" asks Tohlee.

"The shepherds are back in camp, everyone has eaten, and camp is cleaned up. People are starting to gather around the fires."

"Is camp cooking and cleaning for the girls and shepherding for the guys?" asks Tohlee.

"The guys don't do many camp chores except most of the wood gathering. Some girls shepherd and hunt and fish."

"I bet Mateen and Grandfather are settling in next to a fire too," says Eli.

"Do you miss Grandfather or camp?" asks Anoo.

"No, not yet, but I will. No matter how much I like it here I'll still miss my girlfriends and especially my grandfather."

"We're an addition to your family, not a replacement," says Tohlee. "You'll be able to meet the rest of ours. I think Cassie and her boyfriend will be here in a couple days."

"There's also the family the next farm up on our side of the road. We'll have dinner with them soon," adds Eli.

"What do you guys usually do in the evenings?" asks Laurel.

"This is pretty much it in the summer. There's enough work and the days are long enough in the summer that we mostly just relax and regroup before bed. Anoo sometimes goes to town to see his friends. When we have company we stay up and celebrate a little of course," says Eli.

"Do you really know some guys Briana and Teresa would like to meet, Anoo?"

"I do, probably some girls too for your shepherds if any are single."

"A couple are."

"Are you thinking of a get-together before winter?" asks Tohlee.

"I haven't thought that far ahead yet," says Anoo.

"Me either," agrees Laurel. "I have plenty of changes in my life right now, but that is a little selfish. I'd love to see Briana and Teresa with nice guys and women for the men too. We get to our town enough that most of the potential couples have met and things worked or they didn't. Some new interaction would be good for everyone."

"It's something to consider, though there isn't much time this year," says Tohlee, standing up and reaching out her hands to Eli. "Eli, I'm ready for bed with you in it. You guys have a nice rest of the evening too. If you need anything tell me about it in the morning."

"I hope we're that close when we've been together that long," comments Laurel as she gets up and then sits in Anoo's lap.

"So do I, my mesmerizing mermaid."

"I have some practicing to do before I qualify as a mermaid.

Should we think about introducing our various friends?"

"Think about it, sure," says Anoo. "There isn't much time. What would we be trying to do? Are we after just a meeting to give people something to consider over the winter? That could be done by just having a few people go with us back to camp and Briana and Teresa hanging around a little longer than they might otherwise."

"I think it would be too much to expect for anyone to actually couple up, even if Briana and Teresa stayed here or in town a few days," says Laurel.

"Coupling up that quickly could ruin something good that could happen if there wasn't a rush."

"Unlike us," says Laurel, smiling.

"Even we had the equivalent of a handful of dates and afternoons together before we coupled and then coupled up. I guess there could be as much time as we had if we got organized right away."

"Our priority really should be the harvest. What would be better for you, do you think? If you were single, in town, and you learn of the possibility of meeting a couple women new to you. Is the possibility good enough until next year? Or, would you want to get a taste of the possibility before winter?" asks Laurel.

"I'm not sure. By a taste do you mean a meeting at camp or a singles party in town? What about Briana and Teresa?"

"I could be concerned they'd be a little rash and jump into bed first and consider other possibilities later at a town party," considers Laurel.

"It could turn into quite a party with no romantic follow-through."

"That would be my concern," agrees Laurel. "It could turn into just another solstice party when there could be couple potential instead of just coupling potential."

"I'm thinking the couple potential should be encouraged, which points towards an introductory meeting."

"Harvest being a priority and leaning towards couple potential sounds like a meeting at camp. Let's think about this for a few days. What should we do now?" says Laurel, wiggling in Anoo's lap and giving him a kiss.

"Let's go entertain the cats and dogs."

"Good morning, Tohlee."

"Good morning, Laurel!"

"Did you have a nice evening?" asks Laurel, smiling.

"I had a nice evening and a good morning too."

"Oh my, how deliciously naughty of you."

"Well, we've only been together for thirty years or so. May as well indulge when the blood is still stirred up with newness and wonder," says Tohlee, laughing.

"I sincerely hope I can say that after Anoo and I have been together for as long as you and Eli."

"Me too, Laurel, me too. Hey, when you guys go swimming later would you tell Anoo I'd like fish for dinner."

"Of course. Fresh fish sounds good."

After another day of hard but not exhausting work it's time for the young couple to go to the river. They spend some extra time watching the river for fish activity then, before the disturbance of swimming, Anoo readies his willow fly rod. Laurel watches him cast and catch a six-pound pike on his second try. Bringing the fish to shore Anoo kills it with a sudden and sure knife thrust between the eyes. Kneeling next to the fish they both give silent thanks. Thanks for the beauty and strength of this superb predator and for its sustenance. Their thanks are an offer to join its spirit with theirs and is accepted. After Anoo cleans the fish with practiced skill it's time for another swimming lesson. Laurel is athletic and a fast learner. They play a game of tag to help develop her swimming skills and then walk back to the farm.

"Thank you, Anoo, and thank you, Mr. Pike," says Tohlee. "I'll cook him with egg batter and corn flour breading fried in sunflower oil. I think there'll be enough for breakfast too."

"Can I help?"

"Thanks, Laurel, but I'm good. You guys relax or see if Eli needs help finishing anything up. Cassie and Jed will be here tomorrow for a few days," adds Tohlee.

"Hi, Eli."

"Hi, Laurel. Did you guys have a nice swim?"

"We did. I caught Anoo a couple times in our game of tag. I think he let me though and he caught a fish for dinner."

"What kind?"

"A six-pound pike," says Anoo and asks, "Do you need any help?"

"I'm almost done. You guys enjoy yourselves."

"I'll take Laurel for a walk up to your swimming hole. She hasn't been there yet."

Taking their time, they enjoy the walk up to the swimming hole. They watch a mink moving along the shore. After it hunts its way past them, they walk out on a little mud flat that the mink just crossed and look at its tracks. They note the size and the pattern of the tracks as the mink hopped along. Out in the shallow water they see the front halves of several crayfish. They watch as a kingfisher flies by loudly calling out its annoyance at their presence. Turning at the sound of whistling wings they watch two adult mallards and two of their almost grown young set their wings and start to land on the water before seeing them and flying on. At the end of the mud flat they note raccoon and deer tracks—a doe with a fawn. Around a couple of bends and they're at the swimming hole. They see some dimples on the water from feeding fish. They watch as a hummingbird flies across the river and lose sight of it when it lands in a willow.

"What a beautiful spot. This is a funny stump, sticking out of the gravel like this. Did it wash up here?"

"My father put it here," says Anoo, laughing.

"What's so funny?"

"It's here at this angle so he can lean against it when my mother sits on his lap after skinny-dipping. They can be comfortable and look around."

"After skinny-dipping they have a good afternoon like Tohlee had a good evening and morning. That is planning ahead. I'm impressed. We should make a spot like this too, or two. Should we borrow their stump?"

"I'm sure they wouldn't mind but I might. I like it here, but I consider it theirs."

"Okay, what a great place to couple though. I guess I can wait until we entertain the cats and dogs again. But only if you hold me and kiss me and tell me how good it is to have me in your life."

"That would be my pleasure. I like telling the truth, the whole truth, and nothing but the truth."

After continuing their nature walk back to the farm everyone enjoys fresh fish and veggies for dinner before relaxing in their chairs on the porch. They listen to a distant rumble of thunder and Eli says, "It doesn't look like there will be much of a sunset tonight. A nice light and sound show will be fine with me though."

"Will rain interfere with harvest tomorrow?" asks Laurel.

"Not really, well, everything that is drying will have to stay inside. I imagine you guys are prepared for storms but will a severe thunderstorm bother the people at camp?" asks Anoo.

"We stay in the same place every year. Wood structural supports and furniture are left behind for use the next year. Camp is pretty secure for a camp. It can get a little crowded in the tents when it rains. On nice nights half of us sleep outside."

"Where will you and Anoo stay at winter camp?" asks Tohlee.

"We'll probably stay in a cabin with another couple. There aren't enough cabins for us to have our own."

"Do you usually stay with Briana and Teresa?" wonders Tohlee.

"Yes, but Anoo and I couldn't do that. They'd listen and comment and end up making their own little sounds."

After everyone has a good laugh Eli points at the sky. They watch as a thunderhead clears the ridge to the west and a shaft of sun turns the underside of the cloud and the veil of rain coming from it red.

"Beauty surrounds us big and small," says Laurel. "In a thunderclap, in a heartbeat. A flash of lightning, a flickering candle. The canopy of a tall tree swaying in a strong breeze, a blade of grass bending under the weight of morning dew then springing up when a drop falls. A mountain standing tall, the aroma of a rich soil disturbed by a trowel."

"You're a poet, Laurel," says Tohlee. "That was beautiful."

"Thank you. Anoo has inspired me. The warmth and comfort of your home inspires me. Thank you for letting me share this evening and this harvest season with you. Thank you for all the love Anoo has to share. I know his love grows from you two."

"I've always wanted a daughter, Laurel. I hope you don't mind if I fall in love with you too."

"No, Tohlee, not at all," and in a small voice, "I've always wanted a mother." Laurel bursts into tears.

"Laurel! Anoo, you help Laurel into my arms."

"Let's take a walk, Anoo," says Eli.

They get up and walk out of hearing of Tohlee and Laurel where Anoo explains, "Her father died when she was four. I don't think she remembers him well. He went on a hunting and exploring trip and didn't return. Her grandfather thinks he died, not that he chose to stay away. Her mother stays at winter camp. She never got over her hus-band leaving her, which is how she sees it. I think she's always been very distant in a mind gone far way. Laurel was raised more by her grandfather and several motherly women in camp."

"She couldn't be wrapped up in more loving arms. Thanks for telling me," sighs Eli.

After walking around a little it starts to rain. The men go back to their women where Anoo hugs his Laurel.

"I'm sorry I disturbed such a beautiful evening," says Laurel, wip-ing her nose on Anoo's shirt.

"I've always wanted a daughter too, Laurel. Welcome to our fam-ily," Eli says as he kisses her on the head and then heads to bed.

"Thank you and thank you, Tohlee."

"You're welcome, my daughter."

Anoo takes Laurel up to the loft where he holds her until she needs to give back some of the love she's been given.

Chapter Nine

AFTER BREAKFAST AND some harvest work Anoo slips away to find his mother, who's in the house cleaning veggies.

"Why, hello, Anoo, what's up?"

"I wondered if you have some flowers I can pick. I'd like to put some in Laurel's hair before Cassie and Jed get here."

"What a nice thought. Laurel certainly has a sweetheart for a man. I can think of some little yellow and white Johnny-jump-ups that would look great in her black hair."

"When do you think they'll get here?"

"Pretty soon. Cassie let me know they've left town. I'm going to go meet them on the road in just a little bit."

"Hey, where'd you go? What's in your hands?"

"My beautiful Laurel, may I have the pleasure of putting these in your hair?"

"Aspen leaves, flicker feathers, and now flowers. Yes, my gentle man. What a nice thing for you to do." After reflecting Laurel says, "And what a nice feeling. As much as I feel for you already I've still got more falling in love with you to do. I'm going to ask Tohlee if she's still falling in love with Eli. When will Cassie and Jed get here?"

"Pretty soon, an hour maybe."

"Oh, I guess I thought it would be more like dinnertime."

"I think they took care of things at the house and then started walking. We'll all work for a while but I'm sure we'll stop early. Then you'll be the center of attention."

"Should I be nervous?"

"They'll want to get to know you. Not critique you. I think you'll find them very accepting people."

"Can we go down to the river and get cleaned up before they get here? I want to sit naked in the sun when you put flowers in my hair. Hey! hey, wait for me."

"Anoo! It's nice to see you again. What's new?" says Cassie, laughing and hugging him at the same time.

"Aunt Cassie, I'd like you to meet Laurel."

"Hi Cassie."

"Hug me please, Laurel. I've heard so much about you I feel I know you already."

"You have?"

"Tohlee met us a mile down the road and walked with us."

"Oh, that would be more than five minutes to talk. That's more than enough time for my girlfriends and me to cover all the important stuff." Laurel smiles and adds a little abashedly, "I had a bit of an emotional moment last night."

"Five minutes together is all Tohlee and I need too, so I heard about that and more. That moment has been absorbed by this warm and loving family, so don't be concerned. Since Tohlee has told me all your secrets, guess what?"

"I really don't know."

"Tohlee likes you."

"I'm very glad to hear that," says Laurel with a big smile.

"And I have it on good authority, named Tohlee, that Eli likes you too."

"I don't want to cry again."

"What's in your hair? Turn around," says Cassie and then, "You're a beautiful woman and I love these flowers in your hair."

"I said I don't want to cry again," says Laurel laughing and with a little foot stomp for emphasis.

"Let's have the girls work together this afternoon and the guys can do their own thing. Then we can girl talk," says Cassie.

"Hi, Jed," says Anoo, shaking hands. "This is Laurel."

"Hi, Anoo. It's nice to meet you, Laurel."

"Come on, Laurel, let's go," says Cassie.

"I'll see you later, Laurel," says Jed, laughing.

"It's nice to meet you too, Jed," says Laurel over her shoulder as she's being led away.

After an afternoon of work and a swim to clean up, everyone meets at the house. There's too much work to do tomorrow for a late night party, so Eli brings the moonshine out early.

"Did you girls have a nice talk?" asks Jed.

"Yes, did you guys too?" asks Cassie.

"We were too busy working," responds Jed.

"Well, maybe you'll learn to multitask someday," says Cassie with a smile.

"Ouch, I should have seen that one coming," says Jed, feigning having been mortally stabbed.

Everyone laughs, and Cassie says, "I haven't heard how you guys met. I know that Anoo went off to watch the meteor shower. Now here you are, Laurel. Were you wandering around in the woods and suddenly there's Anoo?"

"It was pretty much like that except my grandfather and Mateen put us in proximity to each other."

"I don't know about your grandfather, but I don't see Mateen as a matchmaker," says Cassie.

"I'm surprised too," agrees Eli.

"It seems they did a good job," says Tohlee. "And I didn't know Mateen had such a good friend out there. Did you, Eli?"

"I knew he had contact with the shepherds. I didn't know how much though."

"You're a shepherd, Laurel?" asks Cassie.

"There's a couple dozen of us. About a third stay at winter camp all summer and the rest go up into the hills with the sheep for the summer. I'm more camp help than sheep help."

"You're not stuck up there with a bunch of guys, are you?" asks Cassie.

"Two of my best girlfriends are up there and a couple of the shepherds' women too."

"Where are your friends? Didn't they want to come to town?" asks Cassie.

"They probably would have. I kind of selfishly wanted to focus on Anoo and harvest work and my wonderful hosts."

"You mentioned the possibility of a get-together," remembers Tohlee, and Anoo responds, "I think we're leaning towards having some of my friends from town go back to summer camp with us in October. It would just be a meeting and then looking forward to next year sort of thing."

"That sounds like a good idea. Maybe Jed and I should go as chaperones?" suggests Cassie.

"What's that saying?" asks Eli. "Having the fox guard the henhouse?"

"Laurel, Eli is referring to my getting a little exuberant in my partying. It's only occasional, right, Jed?"

"As long as the definition of occasional is whenever you close the library for the day."

"Oh, stop it. And you love it when I play the demure librarian who has one too many drinks."

"That's certainly true. You know how some people when they move into a new house like to join in every room? Well, Cassie counts each stack of books as a room. And there are a lot of stacks of books in the library."

Laughing Tohlee says, "Let's get back to Laurel and Anoo. Give us an example of the conversations you guys had that caused you two to fall in love."

"I've been considering my girlfriends and when Anoo and I talked about thoughts where the light goes on," says Laurel.

"How were you looking at the light going on?" asks Eli.

"We were saying the light goes on when a new synaptic connection is built in the brain," answers Laurel.

"And then similar ideas and concepts to the idea that caused the light to go on will follow that now established path," continues Anoo.

"And you said you were thinking about your girlfriends, Laurel?" asks Jed.

"Yes, and how Anoo and I came together as a couple."

"How are you going to bring those seemingly disparate things together?" asks Tohlee. "You two becoming a couple, a thought where the light goes on, and your girlfriends?"

"I'm thinking that Anoo and I getting together as a couple is the thought where the light goes on; we're the new synaptic connection," answers Laurel. "If my friends Briana and Teresa get together with a couple guys in town or if a girl from town gets together with a guy from our camp, they will be the similar idea or concept that follows the newly established synaptic connection that Anoo and I created."

"I really like that, Laurel!" says Cassie. "You and Anoo coming together as a couple is a new societal synaptic connection and the future couples will be following your newly created societal path."

"I've got to admit I didn't see that connection coming," says Tohlee with a smile.

"It came out of the blue like a new synaptic connection," says Eli.

"Except for the fertile ground of Laurel's mind," says Jed.

"That's a good point, Jed. A thought where the light comes on doesn't come out of the blue like I just said. It comes from the mental work that's been done prior to the new synaptic connection being made."

162

"Following Laurel's analogy, the work being done before the societal connection made by Laurel and I coming together as a couple would be Mateen and Grandfather meeting and then setting us up to meet," says Anoo.

"I am completely impressed with that line of thought, Laurel," says Tohlee. "What do you think, Eli?"

"I think I'm very impressed and very proud of my two independent perspective holders."

"I'll drink to that," say Jed and Cassie in unison.

"And Laurel, I want to emphasize the 'my two' part; you're a part of our family now too," says Tohlee.

"Here, here," say Jed and Cassie in unison, raising their glasses again.

"I'm going to get dinner going," says Eli.

"Is there anything I can do?" asks Laurel.

"I'm fine, thank you, Laurel. I'm making my honeyed carrots, beets, and pinyon nuts with sausage on the side. You guys are going to go with Tohlee to see her butterfly garden. Which has been a great sphinx moth garden the last few evenings."

"Listening to sphinx moths hovering is a delight," says Anoo.

"Come on, you guys, we're going to the north side gardens," says Tohlee.

At the north side of the house some moths can be seen. Tohlee has set up chairs in a few appropriate spots. The moths quickly go back to what they were doing after everyone takes a seat. In a few minutes there are a half a dozen moths buzzing around the garden. The hummingbirds and butterflies have left for the night. At first everyone just enjoys the sight but then they try to get closer to where the moths are actively feeding. Anoo slowly moves to where his head is inches from some flowers a moth just left. After a couple of minutes another comes by and is buzzing around Anoo's face as it moves from flower to flower. Laurel holds up her hand next to a flower spike until she feels a little breeze from a passing moth. Cassie moves her chair so she's facing the group with flowers on either side of her. They all laugh when she crosses her eyes trying to keep a moth inches in front of her in focus. Tohlee picks up one of her cats that is paying too much attention to the moths and puts it in her lap. After having as many as eight moths flying around the garden everyone moves to the west side of the house where Eli is setting a table. They enjoy their meal as the sky darkens and a couple of packs of coyotes howl to mark the start of their night's hunt. After dinner everyone, including the dogs, walks around the property looking for marauding critters. Then, it's bedtime. Tomorrow's work will start early.

It's another late summer day. A little cooler first thing in the morning than a few weeks ago but it will be hot soon. There will be some afternoon clouds and maybe an evening shower. Many different types of crops are ripening. There's drying, canning, and moving to the root cellar to be done after harvesting and cleaning. There's also time for swimming. Anoo and Laurel are down at their swimming hole. They saw Cassie and Jed come back and now it's their turn. Eli and Tohlee will be going to their pool upstream.

"Cassie and Jed are really nice. Cassie, especially, is full of energy and very accepting. I expected a little bit of a feeling-out process," comments Laurel.

"Part of that is because we're here as a couple. It's not like I'm asking them what they think of you because I'm wondering. I'm already convinced I want you in my life. Cassie is warm and accepting. There are kids who go to the library just to be with her."

"Jed seems like a very steady sort of guy. Have they been together long?"

"Years, I'm not sure how many. For quite a while Cassie was bringing a different guy here every time she came out. After she brought

Jed that's been that."

"They seem like they enjoy being a couple. Tohlee is very accepting too. She's had a stranger move into her home and treats me like a daughter."

"That's because of how warm and considerate you are."

"Thank you, my loving man. You don't have to say nice things to me. I'm already naked."

"It was a statement of fact, not a ploy."

"I think that's what I've been realizing about your family. Everyone is clear and direct. It seems like for you guys ploys and guile are for people who lack ethical values. Manipulating is a sign of deceit not wisdom. Feelings are to share, not use. Perspective is something to grow, not to force on to another. Character is something to have, not a way that a person acts. As parents, did Eli and Tohlee lead by example and proof of perspective or did they have to be authoritarian with you?"

"They say they followed the two and twenty-two rule."

"I'm not familiar."

"They say that some behaviors are forced on parents when they have a two-year-old. If the parents are still doing those things when their child is twenty-two it's a statement of the parents' character, not the child. They say it's more like the two and twelve rule but that doesn't have the same ring to it."

"I like that, and I like the man they've helped to grow into his life. Hey, would you like to use me for your sexual pleasure?"

"I certainly like your individual application of clear and direct," says Anoo, laughing. "Yes, I would. As much because of your personality as your beautiful face and luscious body."

"Cover me up, my love. I want to lie back and feel how good you are in my life."

After much work is accomplished, but before it's too late to enjoy each other's company, everyone is back at the house. First, there's some talk about the day and what will happen tomorrow. Different details but overall more of the same. Then, it's time for more sharing of perspectives.

"I want to hear some more from Anoo and Laurel. More of the kind of things you guys talked about as you fell in love," says Tohlee.

"Could I make a request of Eli first?" asks Laurel.

"Of course, what can I do for you?"

"I guess I'm missing my grandfather. What I'm missing is details. I can feel his love for me and that everything is all right with him but I'm used to more. I'm used to taking his plate after he eats, knowing his belly is full and that he's comfortable. Seeing his smile and leaning my shoulder against his as we watch the fire burn down. I'm wondering what he's doing right now?"

Eli nods his understanding and relaxes back into his chair. After a few minutes he sits up and regains his physical perspective by looking at Tohlee.

"They are sitting on Mateen's back porch. The valley below has been in shadow for almost an hour. A black bear sow and two cubs came out in the open about fifteen minutes ago. They're enjoying watching the cubs play in the water and grub around in the tall grass by the stream. The sow is attentive but much more focused on finding food than the playful cubs. There's been rain showers there the last couple evenings, so this morning they went out looking for boletes. They just finished up a dinner of beef jerky with dried peas and carrots reconstituted in beef broth. The boletes were sautéed in the broth/jerky mix and then served with corn bread. They say peace to us all."

"Thank you, Eli, that's more than I had hoped for."

"That's what I've been wondering about lately," says Anoo, continuing along with Tohlee's request. "Connections, different types of connections. Laurel and I talked about this when we first met. We all know what Eli just did when he communicated with Mateen, but what actually just happened? What connected to what during this communication? Mind connected to mind is more of a statement than an explanation. The time frame was now but it didn't matter Mateen was miles away. How can a mental connection ignore distance and keep time?"

"I think this will be too complicated a conversation to reach a definitive answer tonight. Let's just state our questions and examples now with conclusions coming later, if at all," suggests Tohlee.

"If we're clear now it will be easier to pick up where we left off tomorrow," says Jed in agreement.

"Are there other connections you've been considering, Anoo, besides telepathy?" asks Cassie.

"There's several," he answers. "When I first saw Laurel from a distance I knew right away she was a woman about my age. That was from her movements. As I realized that, she turned and looked right where I was. I was in an aspen stand where she couldn't see me. What connected between us? Did I send something out that you felt, Laurel?"

"I think you must have," answers Laurel. "Otherwise, how would I have known where to look? I did it without thinking. I also sensed you were male. And what happened when we looked at each other from a distance after we said good-bye for the evening? We looked each other in the eye from a distance but it was like we were looking in each other's eyes from two feet apart. Distance didn't matter then either."

"Eyes are the window to the soul," says Cassie. "That isn't an explanation. It's just a vague statement saying something out of the ordinary is going on."

"When eye contact is made with a wild animal they immediately know that the contact is with something that has awareness and intent. What is substituting for eye contact in Anoo and Laurel's example?" wonders Eli.

"You started with Eli and Mateen's telepathic connection, Anoo. What about empathy?" asks Jed. "Does empathy come from the same place as telepathy? Telepathy being a more precise form of the same connection perhaps? Or do they come from two different places, two different processes?"

"When I leave my body in a dream state what connects my awareness to my body?" wonders Laurel.

"When I become aware of something of out-of-the-ordinary interest as I walk around, what part of me senses that thing when it's out of sight?" Anoo continues. "If it's a rock I can't smell or hear it. I know I've done the same with animals because I've done it with fish in the river. An errant breeze or a sound that doesn't fully register with me couldn't be the reason."

"When we become aware we're dreaming what becomes aware of what?" asks Tohlee. "How can we be asleep and then become aware of what we're already doing? Or, how can we wake our sleeping selves up when we're actively dreaming?"

"How can we be asleep and dreaming at the same time?" asks Cassie and then, "What is asleep and what is dreaming? The mind in each case and at the same time. The activity of dreaming takes place during sleep. That's not an explanation, that's another vague statement saying something out of the ordinary is going on."

"When I become aware that I'm sleeping and sit up, sitting in my own body, I can touch Anoo and that part of him sits up; what part of me did I touch Anoo with and what part of him sat up?"

"Whoa, are you saying that happened?" asks Anoo.

"Last night. I'll do it again when I can. I think you were too deeply asleep to become fully aware of me. We'd worked hard all day, there was the activity of meeting Jed and Cassie, plus indulging in naked pleasures. I ended up lying back down and going to sleep like you did."

"This is such an interesting conversation but also hard to grasp. I think we should regroup for a few minutes," Tohlee suggests.

"I do want to offer what may lead to a conclusion in the long run," says Eli.

"Please do, my love. I wasn't trying to cut the conversation off."

"I am, and I think we all are, people who think heart and mind, body and soul, reason and feelings shouldn't be considered separate in this life. Are the seeming dichotomies we've been talking about caused by a separation within us that we are trying to resolve? Perhaps the separation between body and soul while here on Earth?" asks Eli and says as a definition, "Soul being the part of us that continues on after death."

"Is there a connection needed in each of us to resolve the dichotomies we perceive that we have? Dichotomies we're aware of because of our own efforts at directness and clarity?" asks Tohlee.

"Are these dichotomies a permanent truth, or are they a flaw that needs correcting? Maybe an effect of disjoining? If we were perceiving from our soul would these seeming dichotomies, as seen from a physical perspective, go away?" asks Anoo.

"Now I definitely need a break as Tohlee suggested," says Jed.

As the sun sets everyone sits and thinks and sips. Clouds have built enough so that the sunset colors are quiet entertainment. Hues change as clouds move and the sun drops. It doesn't look like there will be much rain, if any. After time to reflect on their conversation there's the distraction of eating with accompanying small talk. When things are cleaned up, instruments come out. Jed is a guitar player and Eli the mandolin. There are drums and Cassie is singing. After playing for a while Laurel and Anoo dance. When Tohlee and Eli start to dance Jed and Cassie slow the music down. It doesn't take long for the slow dancing to cause the couples to say good night.

The next day is much the same as the day before. Good weather with an increased chance of a storm in the evening. Good work mixed with time to swim, time to be friends with a common goal. Anoo finds and shows everyone a four-foot-long bull snake with a bulge in its belly. Bull snakes have to eat too, and it was probably a rodent that would have raided their crops anyway. Of course, rodents have to eat, but so do people. Later, Eli calls everyone's attention to a large flock of blackbirds. They circle around the farm but don't land. As they circle everyone watches as their wings flapping causes the blue of the sky to flicker with the black of wings. Anoo likes to count the animals he sees and makes a quick assessment. Ten birds take up this much space, a hundred that much. He decides that a couple thousand in the flock is a good guess. In the evening it's time for reflection and relaxation. Everyone is back on the west-facing porch watching the sun set. There are too many clouds for good color. If there's a shower it will be welcome. As they settle in to their chairs Tohlee asks, "What else did you guys talk about as you fell in love?"

"I'd like to follow up on our thoughts on the *light goes on* conversation," says Anoo.

"Okay, what have you thought about?" says Tohlee.

"I'm thinking that a thought where the light goes on is more than the thought itself and more than the meaning of the concept that caused the light to go on. It is also a description of a physical event that happens in the brain," says Anoo.

"That's what I was saying when I said it is when a new synaptic connection is made in the brain," says Laurel.

"That's right. I'm adding on and saying that synaptic connection is an opportunity to become aware of where our perceptions are coming from. That light is an opportunity to become aware of our available levels of consciousness. The levels of ourselves we're not using when we're being sexual or heartfelt or compassionate," explains Anoo.

"Are you saying that when the fire of the mind is lit, the mind becomes as perceptive an organ as the heart?" asks Laurel.

"I am. Different value systems are involved; each organ of perception has its own pluses and minuses. Still, the mind, lit up by electrical activity, can evaluate situations like the heart can."

"Each organ of perception has its own pluses and minuses. So, just as with reason and feeling, the heart and mind are meant to work together, complement each other, not be exclusive of each other," says Laurel.

"Yes, and in working together, they will reach an area that neither could separately," says Anoo.

"A symbiotic relationship that allows the feelings of the heart to be tempered with the ethical constructs of the mind. The pettiness, vindictiveness, and envy, for example, which can be felt in the heart can be tempered with the ethics of the mind. The lack of compassion that the mind may have can be tempered with the compassion of the heart," says Laurel.

"You guys must have had some interesting conversations," says Cassie.

"Interesting and with a lot of potential to build on," says Tohlee.

"I'd like to jump over to connections now," says Jed. "Does anyone have any thoughts to add to Anoo's talk of connections?"

"I've been thinking about the time and distance Anoo mentioned. How telepathic or empathic communication takes place over distances without any more time being involved than if the communication was between two people sitting next to each other," Eli comments. "Mateen has set me up with telepathic communications that are designed to wait for me to be ready. I've been unavailable to communicate with him for one reason or another like when I'm talking to someone else or indulging in naked pleasures. When I'm available I can find contact and communication from Mateen. That communication must have been waiting out there somewhere for me."

"Waiting where?" asks Tohlee.

"I don't know. I've done the same or, intended to do the same in Mateen's direction. We've never talked about whether I was successful or not. He might have received the communication or I might not have put it in the right place because I'm not sure where that place is."

"You don't know where the communication is stored. Mateen, though, has left the communication right up against where he usually connects with you. He would say it's stored on the edge of telepathic communication with you. Waiting for you to be ready to make a connection," says Tohlee.

"I think that's right and that means the place the communication is stored is where the telepathic connection is made. The telepathic connection is mind to mind. That still doesn't nail down how the connection works. It's a connection between two physical minds in a way that can disregard time and/or distance," responds Eli.

"Let's keep going. Are we accepting that telepathic communication can reach beyond time as it can reach beyond distance?" asks Anoo.

"Yes, we are," Tohlee answers.

"I don't know if this will help, but Mateen has told me about an experience of his that is beyond nonlinear time," says Eli. "He considers nonlinear time a fact because of what happened to him."

"Would he mind if you tell us the story?" asks Laurel.

"I'm sure he wouldn't. He was driving a truck while working for the city of Denver. They have a maintained road going from a reservoir and power plant down to the city. His job was to check the power lines and the road for repair needs. The night before this happened he woke up after having a very clear dream. He remembered every detail of the dream and went back to sleep. He remembered every detail again on waking up in the morning. Later that morning, while he was driving, a big piece of ice fell off a tall tree by the side of the road and smashed his windshield. As the ice fell he remembered his dream. The piece of ice twisted and turned as it fell just like in his dream. He couldn't react to the situation, even with the foreknowledge, fast enough to avoid having his windshield smashed. He thinks the dream caused him to be calm enough after the collision to keep the truck on the road and not go off a steep embankment where he could easily have been killed."

"That's an incredible story. I think it will take me a little while to digest," says Laurel.

"I need to stretch some," says Anoo and adds, "Keep talking. I'm listening."

"I need to also, Anoo. I can't bend and reach like a youngster anymore," says Jed.

"Nonlinear time is hard to imagine," says Tohlee. "Can a person feel hurt before they fall? Or can they skip the hurt of falling and jump to the end of the healing process?"

"Maybe we should look at this from a feeling standpoint," Cassie suggests, "from a feeling of forgiveness standpoint. Think about two estranged people. They were close and then something happened to drive a wedge between their friendship. Perhaps something is learned, giving a different take on the issue they were having or maybe time just passes—anyway, forgiveness happens. With forgiveness there's a cascade of feelings, the end result of which might be that there was never a problem between the two. No problem, at least from the standpoint of how they feel about each other. Do you think that's an example of nonlinear time?"

"Personally, I don't think I'd forget what happened to cause the problem. I think I'd just get over it," says Eli.

"I'm not saying forget. I'm saying the emotional trauma of an abruptly ended friendship would be as though the trauma had never been," says Cassie.

"I'm following Cassie." Eli gets up and moves around to keep from getting chair stiff.

"I think it would depend on the perspective of the individuals involved," says Laurel. "You guys try to be clear and direct in all you do. When you're communicating, indulging in naked pleasures, or causing someone to feel good about themselves. It doesn't matter, you're intending your actions."

"When we think back on our lives we remember our actions as much as our feelings," says Tohlee in agreement.

"Now consider two friends who live their individual lives focusing on their feelings," says Laurel. "Unlike you guys, these people hold the value system that their feelings can be caused by others. When they look back on their lives they remember how they felt more than what caused them to feel. For people with that perspective forgiveness would be like a new start. It would be as though their problem never existed. Feelings changed and so their past may as well have too."

"That is certainly a different take on 'time heals all wounds,'" comments Jed.

"I think that example counts as much toward the reality of non-linear time as Mateen's experience. An experience that was clear and concise due to his perspective on life," says Eli.

"Or was it clear and concise because of the effort his spirit guides were making to contact him," suggests Anoo.

"You're saying spirit guides to represent a phenomenon that others having a different perspective would term angels or the ancestors?" asks Jed.

"That's right, Jed."

"This subject of connections has connections I never imagined when Anoo originally brought it up," says Tohlee.

"I was thinking about where the connections are made," says Anoo.

"Which connections and where are they made?" prompts Jed.

"We're saying telepathic connections are made mind to mind. I think empathetic connections are too," continues Anoo.

"Empathy is heartfelt," says Laurel.

"Heartfelt, yes, but I think the communication of those feelings is done through the mind like telepathy," explains Anoo.

"That is pointing towards a similar process of communication for each," says Cassie.

"Is anyone thinking anything different?" asks Eli. After no response but heads shaking no he says, "We'll go with that for now. If anyone comes up with something different let everyone else know."

"What about feeling like someone is looking at you?" asks Jed.

"I was focused on Laurel through my eyes and thinking about what I was seeing," says Anoo.

"I felt Anoo's attention on me in my mind, or around my mind. If he directed his attention on me now I'd feel warmth in my heart too. That would be after I realized it was Anoo and not where the original contact was realized," says Laurel.

"The eye contact or connection that transcends distance is in the mind also," adds Anoo.

"Are we just talking about where sensorial information is processed?" asks Tohlee and adds as an explanation, "Sensorial contact is from the body but processed in the mind."

"We're looking at examples of connections that come from outside our physical selves but then are processed in our mind," says Eli.

"Is that processing in the mind or in the soul? The soul perhaps has an overview of what we are doing here in the physical," Anoo wonders.

"Does the needed or missing connection we mentioned yesterday correlate with a lack of individual connection with that part of us we call soul and the everyday parts of us?" asks Cassie.

"When people strive for contact with an overlord termed God are people actually striving for more contact with the part of themselves that continues on after death and possibly has an overview of our physical lives? Compared to a deity that can solve our problems for us?" asks Jed.

"A soul-level overview could solve our problems without being an overview from a supreme being," says Anoo.

"Is our soul what's awake in a dream when we're asleep?" asks Tohlee.

"Is our soul what connects us telepathically?" asks Eli.

"I can envision souls being beyond time and distance," says Cassie.

"This is tough stuff to wade through," comments Laurel. "Do you think Mateen or Grandfather could help us work through this?"

"I'm guessing we'd be past their ability to explain," Eli suggests. "I'm not sure, but I think they'd be working from experience toward explanation as we are. We'll get them caught up on this when they're here and find out then."

"When they're here!" Laurel sits up straight.

"Whoops, Eli," says Tohlee, laughing.

"Yes, Laurel, Grandfather is thinking of coming here with Mateen to meet everyone and see you," says Eli. "I wasn't going to say anything until he said for sure. He wouldn't stay for the harvest, just a visit."

"When he went back to camp he could tell everyone there about a possible meeting in October with some friends from town," says Anoo.

"I didn't mean to hide this from you, Laurel. I was just waiting for confirmation."

"That's fine, Eli. The possibility of seeing him sooner than October made my heart jump. I miss him more than I've been admitting to myself."

"Your life has been lived in contact with him and he's had a large effect on your perspective," Tohlee comments. "Are we good with our connection talk for now? I think I'm ready to let this conversation sink in with dinner and moonshine."

"Moonshine will help loosen us up physically," says Cassie.

"Tomorrow afternoon I'll get the sweat lodge fired up. Some steamy heat and a jump in the river always helps tired muscles and stiff joints," says Anoo.

"I'll have to go back to town tomorrow morning but I'll be back in the evening. I need to check in with work and I'll stop by the library too," says Jed.

"Tell them I'll be away for a couple more days. I'm really enjoying this visit and getting to know Laurel," says Cassie.

"I am enjoying everyone's company," says Laurel. "Tohlee, is there anything I can do for you? I need to get up and move anyhow."

"Dinner is cooking, you already set the table, everything is good," answers Tohlee.

"Can I brush your hair for you? I love to brush Briana and Teresa's hair as we relax around the fire in the evening."

"Oh my, that would be fantastic. What a sweetheart you are."

"I'll be next," volunteers Cassie with a smile.

"Let's wait until after dinner," suggests Tohlee. "The guys are going to go do some patrolling with the dogs then, aren't you, Eli?"

"Yes, we'll be on the lookout for raccoons especially and sometimes the bears seem to be a little bolder when it's cloudy and the night is darker than usual."

"They choose which conditions are best to raid the fields?" asks Laurel.

"They do," says Anoo. "The raccoons and bears are free to move along the river under the cottonwoods. If they come up on the bench the farm is on, the dogs are free to go into defensive mode. They're more likely to risk the dogs on a dark and stormy night."

"Ooooh, how scary," says Cassie, laughing. "These guys know the farm they live on and animal behavior, Laurel. Don't be misled by the joking."

"Yes, they do. I've been very impressed by their expertise and am learning a lot."

"Do you know how a raccoon climbs down a tree?" asks Anoo.

"Very carefully?" answers Laurel.

"Well, yes," says Anoo, smiling. "But I was referring to how they come down the trunk head first, so they can look around for danger. When they're about ten feet from the ground they turn around butt first so they can scramble back up the tree quickly if there's something down there they missed."

"I'm picturing a mother raccoon going down the tree with a handful of little ones behind her copying her every movement," says Laurel, laughing. "It's good for parents to pass on their wisdom to their children."

After dinner the girls start their hair brushing time and the guys and dogs go to look around. After a while the dogs can be heard barking and snarling with a couple of yells from the men besides. Laurel stops her brushing to listen. Tohlee says with a smile that there's no need for Laurel to stop brushing her hair. She explains that by the sound of things the men and dogs found some raccoons but everything should be fine. The yells they're hearing are just to keep the dogs from hurting a raccoon. If the guys had run into a bear they would hear Eli and Anoo's yells cracking like a whip and focused right at the bear. The dogs' barking would be much more excited too.

Chapter Ten

AFTER BREAKFAST JED leaves for town and everyone else starts the day's harvest. The morning's weather is good and a lot gets done. As afternoon starts to shift to evening Anoo goes down by the river to start a fire and put the cover on the sweat lodge frame. When the fire is burning hot he puts some rocks charred black from earlier use in the fire and covers them up with fresh wood. He goes back to see how the work is progressing. On the way, he sees that the sky is darkening and the wind is picking up. Laurel is helping Eli move the produce that's on the drying racks into the barn because of the threatening sky. Tohlee and Cassie must be working in the house. Anoo helps move the last of the drying veggies into the barn. Eli goes to the house while Anoo and Laurel watch the coming storm.

"I like to watch the gusts of wind move across the fields," says Anoo.

"Let's go out and feel them," Laurel suggests, taking Anoo's hand.

Out in the pasture they watch for particularly strong gusts.

"Look at that one!" Anoo points across the pasture.

"This way," calls out Laurel and they run to get in the gust's path.

"It's almost here!" she says and then they both feel the gust hitting them in the face. As the gust of air keeps going they turn and watch it pushing its way through the tall grass of the pasture.

"When I see the gusts coming and they say hello with a blast to my face, I feel like naming them as I watch them leave," says Anoo.

"The way they move here and there it's as though they have their own personalities," agrees Laurel.

"They are their own entity over time and distance," says Anoo.

"So are thunderstorms," Laurel points out.

"I like the details of the individual movements of the gusts compared to the more lumbering thunderstorms."

When they see another particularly strong one they both race across the pasture to intercept it. They feel the gust on their faces and race after it trying to keep up. Stopping to catch their breath they watch the gust reach the end of the pasture and then rise to shake the branches on one side of a cottonwood.

"They are fun to play with," says Anoo.

"This reminds me of trying to catch snowflakes on my tongue," says Laurel. "Just on a lot bigger scale."

After some more racing around the pasture and meeting up with some interesting gusts they go down to the river. Anoo pulls the heated rocks from the fire with some strong forked sticks cut for this use. He adds more rocks and wood to the fire. Using the forked sticks again they move the hot rocks into the sweat lodge and close it back up. They need to wait for the next batch of rocks to heat up before the lodge is ready for a sweat. They get naked and jump in the river. After swimming around they've rinsed away the workday's sweat and are feeling nice and cool. Back at the fire they move a couple more rocks into the lodge and climb in. Anoo has already put a pot of water and some little bundles of sage in the lodge. Sprinkling some water on the rocks causes the lodge to quickly go from warm to steamy hot. After playfully slapping each other with the sage bundles Anoo and Laurel run down to the river and jump in. They relish the feeling of the abrupt temperature change on their skin and go back to the fire. More rocks are placed into the lodge and more rocks and wood into the fire. They go back in the lodge. It's even warmer this time. Anoo puts some sage on the new dry rocks to smolder. When the scent permeates the steamy air Laurel sprinkles more water on the rocks. Now it's really hot. Anoo sits behind Laurel. He moves her hair off her back and rubs her shoulders. His fingers knead in deep to her muscles as they slip over her wet, clean skin. He watches the little semicircles his fingers make in her skin move in front of his fingertips. Laurel indulges in the wonderful feeling until she gets too hot. Leaning back against Anoo she takes his hands in hers and puts them on her breasts for a slippery squeeze and then says, "River please." They go back to the cool water, then the fire and the lodge, and more massaging. A couple more cycles and they walk naked to the barn for clean clothes. Going into the house, they offer to make dinner while Eli, Tohlee, and Cassie enjoy their sweat time. After everyone has had their sweat and with dinner almost ready they relax on the porch. A few minutes later the dogs go racing down the lane barking. Soon, they're back with Jed. He goes down to the river for a quick swim and then it's dinnertime. Over dinner Jed talks about what's been happening in town. Everything is fine at his work and the library, so he can stay a couple more days.

Then it's time for drinks and more talk.

"Where are we on our connection conversation?" asks Eli.

"I have been thinking about how to reinforce out-of-the-ordinary connections," says Anoo.

"Do you mean how to have the connections more often so they become more familiar?" asks Eli.

"Yes, when I first moved toward an exceptional rock specimen without knowing why I was going where I was, I hardly realized what I had done. It happened another time or two and I started paying more attention."

"It happened as though coming from something outside yourself?" asks Laurel.

Nodding in agreement Anoo says, "After thinking about what happened I wanted to see if it was something I did. First, I put myself in a similar situation. By myself, wandering around out in the scrub. I tried to remember how I felt when I changed direction without knowing why. I asked myself what I was doing before I started to move."

"You wanted to make an unfamiliar process familiar and so repeatable," states Laurel.

"That's right. I realized I had become immersed in doing what I was doing. I wasn't thinking about school or girls in town or how much time I had before I needed to be home for dinner. I was very clear-headed, without distractions and not actively looking for rocks. That's why I was there but I was actively walking quietly with an awareness of where I was. I felt like I wanted to go in a different direction. At first I talked myself out of the impulse because I was expecting more of a 'there's a nice crystal over there' type of motivation."

"Expecting too much awareness in a process you were still unfamiliar with," comments Laurel.

"I ignored my expectations and just wanted to have the experience again. When I did, I thought about what I had done just from a memory standpoint. I looked back where I had been. I walked back a few hundred yards before walking over to where I found the specimen. When I did I felt like I was realizing why I did what I did a little more. There was more memory in me, of my own actions during the event than I was aware of initially."

"You felt the realization of why without actively knowing why?" asks Laurel.

"I was still acting outside the awareness of myself for the most part. After repeating the process multiple times, I became more familiar with the mental clarity I had before and as I moved. Not so much clearly focused as open to possibilities. I learned to recognize feelings that were motivations and separate them from feelings that were distractions."

"What was the difference?" asked Jed.

"Not so much the feeling itself but the openness to possibilities I was perceiving. With a clear mind the motivation that caused me to move was what I was after. Without a clear mind, open to possibilities, the same motivation with the same feeling of *this is important* could bring up a memory, or thoughts of what I was going to do in school the next day. After more repetition, the process became increasingly familiar, the mind-set more recognizable, the distractions easier to ignore. I'd have a feeling of certainty about what I was about to do. This grew to where I could tell friends I was with what I was going to find later in the day. I could start walking in a different direction and tell them, 'Come with me. I'm going to find a nice crystal over here.' When I was almost there I would let them go in front of me to see the specimen first."

"What was awake before you became aware of what you were actively doing? What led you to your own expected conclusion?" asks Tohlee.

"And I say the answer is me," says Anoo.

"Which makes sense when you can connect what seems to be different parts of yourself. When you're not connected what you're saying is just the terminology of an explanation," says Cassie.

"That's why it's important to explore those times when an individual finds themselves out at the edge of their awareness. Bring those events more into your awareness and the edge of your awareness of self grows outward," says Eli.

"Out toward a part of one's self that has been disjoined," says Laurel.

"I want to shift the conversation a little," says Cassie.

"Please do. I'm too interested in the conversation for a break," says Jed.

"I think I do the same thing Anoo is talking about doing with rock specimens," Cassie says, "but I do it with children at the library."

"Interesting expansion of the phenomenon. Please explain," Jed encourages.

"I've gone to the far end of the library without knowing why and found a kid with a problem that needed some one-on-one talking. I've done the same walking down to the river when it wasn't my time for a break. I don't think it's because I heard a sniffle from quiet tears that I didn't quite realize was a sniffle."

"I think that sounds like the same idea. I don't mean to suggest that looking for rock specimens is the only way to reach that level of awareness. It's what worked for me," explains Anoo.

"I do see a difference between connecting with a kid with a

problem and an inanimate object like a rock," says Tohlee. "The kid could have given some body language or facial expression that you keyed in on, except you said you've done that with kids down by the river. Still, connecting with the inanimate rock has its own mysteries, I'm thinking."

"My question is more of a shift of conversation and goes back to nonlinear time," says Laurel. "I am starting with the idea that a person can perceive away from the body. Can a person send their awareness out on a string and connect to a future version of themselves?"

"Or, is that connection a telepathic thing that happens in the mind. A connection with something that is our self but is currently disjointed and has an overview of our self in our daily life?" asks Eli.

"And is that soul or do we end up with an overview of our self, in our mind, because of the many choices we make in our lives?" asks Jed.

"Would regret help build that overview if it isn't soul?" asks Tohlee. "We wouldn't need an overview if we didn't make mistakes."

"I think we've reached a need for a break so we can bring the ramifications of these various ideas into our ability to verbalize," says Eli.

"We have been talking about these ideas as though they're part of an out-of-the-ordinary process. And yet, the process of rejoining parts of our self through unfamiliar connections is very similar to thinking about a concept until we understand it well enough to be able to explain it to others," says Tohlee.

"Either way we're assessing, exploring, trying to understand with our minds conceptually, while we use our hearts to keep from going astray. We're using our thoughts to reach out and our feelings as a moral compass," says Cassie.

"The goal being to reach a familiarity, a clarity, or level of understanding, so we can repeat an individual experience by choice and to communicate a newly understood concept to others," says Laurel.

"Okay, now I need to regroup," says Jed.

As a few raindrops start to fall the gusty wind from earlier returns.

There is a brief but intense rainstorm with some distant flashes of lightning and rumbling thunder. The winds die down as the storm passes and the guys go out on another check for marauding critters. There are a couple of alerts from the dogs but nothing confrontational. Afterward, everyone decides it's time for a good night's sleep so they'll be ready for another day's work tomorrow.

The morning is clear and it looks like the unsettled weather that brought yesterday evening's rainstorm has passed. Eli and Anoo check the hay meadow and decide they should wait until tomorrow to cut it as the tall grass is still wet. That means harvesting more veggies today. Everyone settles in to what is becoming an enjoyable routine of hard work. At one point Jed, Laurel, and Anoo are out in a garden bed while everyone else is in the house. They're finishing up a couple of rows of beans. The pintos are going to the drying racks, the yellow and green will be canned, and the purple eaten fresh. They'd can the purples too but they lose their color during the blanching process.

All of a sudden all three stand up and turn around as a terrified shriek cuts through the air. They see two birds locked together and spiraling downward. One is shrieking and the other is struggling to keep from plummeting to the ground. As soon as they hit, the shrieks are cut off.

"What was that!" asks Laurel.

"That was a sharp-shinned hawk taking a flicker," answers Anoo. He calls to stop the dogs, who have come charging from their shady rest spot at the sound.

"They're about the same size. I'm surprised the hawk took a bird as big as it is," says Jed.

"It could barely keep a hold of the flicker and keep from falling," says Anoo. "As soon as it got to the ground and had some leverage it killed the flicker easily."

"It can't fly away with it, can it?" asks Laurel.

"I wouldn't think so. I imagine the hawk is cutting open the body cavity and eating the guts right now. They do that first in case something bigger comes along and tries to steal their kill."

"That shrieking could bring in a predator from some ways away," comments Jed.

"Just like the dogs did," says Laurel in agreement.

"I wonder if it will pluck and eat the rest of it or be happy with the guts?" says Anoo. "It's not going to want to stay on the ground for long."

"Was it playing with the flicker like a cat with a mouse?" asks Laurel.

"I wouldn't think so," says Anoo. "It would have stopped the shrieking sooner if it could because of the concern of other predators."

"I wonder if it is a young hawk not sure of its own capabilities," says Jed.

"That's a possibility," says Anoo.

"It almost bit off more than it could chew, so to speak," says Laurel.

"I bet it can't finish the whole bird and still fly away," comments Anoo.

"Wouldn't it stop eating before it's too full to fly?" Laurel asks him.

"Maybe at this time of year. But, then again, maybe at this time of year it wouldn't. Maybe it's a young bird on its own for the first time and so very hungry and might gorge itself."

"Young, and so inexperienced at knowing what bird to take and what ones to let go by. Also, young and not experienced at knowing how full it can be and still fly," says Jed.

"I watched two bald eagles eat on a winter-killed carcass once. They must have been really hungry because when two coyotes came in to the carcass they flew about a hundred feet, barely getting off the ground, before landing in sagebrush," says Anoo.

"I'm surprised two balds would be concerned with a couple coyotes," comments Laurel.

"I think that was due to their being full too. I think they'd have stayed and eaten if they weren't stuffed," says Anoo. "I've seen a golden square off with a coyote. It didn't last long. The coyote approached the eagle while it was on the ground; the eagle probably had made a kill. As the coyote approached the golden hopped up a foot in the air and spread its wings. The coyote immediately backed off and left."

"Predators can't risk injury in close fights. They have too much trouble making kills when they're healthy," says Jed.

"That's where I think predators playing with their prey comes from," says Anoo. "They do play. But I think that cat-and-mouse play starts with the concern of being bitten. Even a coyote wouldn't want a mouse biting it on the lip and holding on. When they quickly grab a mouse and flip it away they're trying to disable the mouse so it can't bite. Once they get the mouse to that point they'll play with it."

"Unless they're hungry; then they'll just eat it to get it into their stomach, where it's relatively secure. Like the hawk eating the flicker's guts," says Jed.

"And mice can be aggressive," says Anoo. "I was out walking on a moonlit winter's night. I saw a mouse come onto the crusty snow from a clump of grass. It was running over to another clump to get back under the snow. I thought I could cut it off so I ran toward it. The mouse knew I could get to it before it could get to the grass clump, so it turned and hopped up a foot in the air for several jumps. It came right at me. I was so surprised I stopped running and the mouse turned and ran to the grass clump."

"Jed, should I be concerned that Anoo is afraid of a little bitty mouse?" Laurel asks with a smile.

"I definitely think so," says Jed, laughing.

"I'm going back to work. I don't deserve to have such brutal and cutting words aimed at me," says Anoo with feigned indignation.

When evening comes around everyone is back on the porch ready for some moonshine, relaxing, and interesting talk. The sharp-shinned hawk taking the flicker made for a good story earlier. The sweat lodge was once again welcome relief from the bending and reaching of harvesting veggies. The harvest is going well. The short rainstorm the night before didn't slow things down. Food for winter and barter is accumulating at a goodly rate. After some small talk Jed is wondering about a comment Eli made.

"I'd like to talk more about the edge of awareness Eli talked about."

"How so Jed?" asks Eli.

"I want to try to define the term. I want to call it the edge of awareness the individual has of their own capability."

"I want to say the edge where the magic of timing lives," says Tohlee.

"I like the edge where coincidence becomes destiny," says Cassie.

"I'll go with where superstition cedes to clarity," says Eli.

"Are we also talking about the physical limits of the senses?" asks Laurel.

"We are when we're talking about moving the ability to sense away from the body on a string of self," says Anoo.

"There's a physical connection when we're talking about pushing the physical limits of the body beyond one's perceived limits," says Jed.

"Okay, so the edge of awareness can be an edge of physical muscular capability, physical sensorial capability, or the edge of awareness of what an individual actually is beyond our direct physical being."

"Well said, Laurel. I think that edge should be pushed outward. The more understanding of our capabilities and what we, as individuals, are, the better," says Anoo.

"Awareness being the key. We're not saying individuals can't expand themselves by following their heart. We're saying that use of the word 'heart' is actually representing a lack of conscious understanding or awareness. It's not pointing to a method of growing as a person we're not tapping into because of our choice to be clear and direct. We all put things into the back of our minds and have an answer come to us. We all feel our way through life," says Eli.

"We feel our way through life after we learn and communicate as much as possible. Hopefully giving our feelings a stronger base," says Cassie.

"We think conscious awareness leads to empowerment, opportunity, and freedom," says Tohlee.

"Thinking, learning, and communicating doesn't take away from feeling. They complement feeling," says Jed.

"Body and soul, heart and mind, feeling and reason are to be brought together. They aren't efficient separately just like the heart can't survive without the brain or the brain without the heart," says Laurel.

"Let's go back to the overview we mentioned before," says Eli. "We're thinking an individual has an overview of themselves. Sort of an 'if I hadn't made mistakes' overview; if we functioned with all the awareness we're capable of we'd be acting from that overview. We're also thinking there is an overview given by our soul. An overview that can be grown with our own thoughts and feelings of enough quality."

"Those two overviews may be the same thing," says Jed.

"Are we sure these overviews don't include the perspective of a supreme being? Are we taking a supreme being out of our perspective in a way we're all comfortable with?" asks Tohlee.

"We should try to define our terms here," Eli suggests. "I think Anoo can start us off."

"Okay, I'll give my version and we'll go from there," says Anoo. "I think there are two different phenomenon that often get mixed together conceptually into one supreme being. The first is the creator of the universe. That would be the entity that is behind the singularity that started the big bang. How that entity learned to cause itself to be in a physical world I don't know. The physical world created by that big bang is about fifteen billion years old. The entity that created it did not hang around studying geology and astrophysics for almost fifteen billion years before creating his greatest singular achievement of life—Homo sapiens. That entity has created and seen thousands

188

of intelligent species begin, thrive, and pass away over that fifteen billion years. Thousands of intelligent species includes trillions of intelligent individuals. The supreme being contains all those lives and experiences. Is everyone okay with this so far?"

"We've talked about this before, so I think we're okay," replies Jed as everyone else nods in agreement.

"That entity commonly termed as God gave dominion of life on Earth to Homo sapiens. That dominion over life on Earth includes humans themselves. That entity made us in its image. Its image of itself is as a self-determinate being not a reflection in a mirror. We are responsible for our own futures, destiny, fate, or whatever you want to call it. No great authority figure is going to bail us out of troubles we cause ourselves or troubles caused by living on this sometimes violent planet. We are responsible for ourselves. Everyone still okay?"

"You're doing well, keep going," says Laurel.

"The second phenomenon is a subset of the first and able to act separately. It is made from human consciousness. That being has seen billions of humans come and go, has encompassed thousands of languages and societies over people's time on Earth. That accumulation of human consciousness is also commonly referred to as God. I'm making a distinction between those two groupings of life experience. The first I'll term the Universal God. The second the God in human consciousness. Help me pay attention to what I'm saying so I don't confuse the two."

"Keep going, Anoo, you're doing fine," Laurel encourages.

"I'm going to be talking about the God in human consciousness now. I'll start with where does that God exist? In human consciousness. Where did human consciousness come from? Humans, as far as I know, have always had that consciousness overview with them. When we were tribal people there was a tribal consciousness. When people lived in isolated villages there was a village consciousness. Going back to before Homo sapiens there was a pack-type consciousness like what a troop of chimpanzees has these days. It's shown by the way chimpanzees move as a group to forage or commit acts of war. Acting as a group, living within a tribe, creates that overview of consciousness."

"I want to interject," says Tohlee. "I want a better definition of what this human consciousness is. You've given examples of groups of people having this consciousness, showing that consciousness has been around as long as humans, but not so much what it is."

"That consciousness is an inclusive view of all of humanity. It's the memories from humans who lived long ago. It's the societal subtleties contained in different languages. It's all the different religions," answers Anoo.

"You're saying it's the inclusive accumulation of human experience in the same way the freedoms of this country's constitution are inclusive. Those freedoms apply to all Homo sapiens regardless of gender, race, religion, sexual orientation, or language spoken just as the consciousness you're talking about includes all humans," says Laurel.

"That's right, I'm also saying it includes the experiences of individual lives after death. Life after death is a part of human consciousness as the life of humans continues on after death, from my perspective."

"I think we all agree. I think we're all following you, Anoo. You're doing an excellent job of saying this succinctly," compliments Cassie.

"Human consciousness was split at some time in humanity's past. I don't know how or why. The result is that we see the God in human consciousness as separate from us the same way that the Universal God must be separate from us if we are supposed to have dominion over ourselves and all other life on Earth. That perspective of being separated from the God in human consciousness is an error. The God in human consciousness is us. It is a product of human lives. Seeing that God in human consciousness as something separate from us is an error in perspective. The God in human consciousness can't quell volcanoes or tsunamis any more than people can. The perceived split between the God in human consciousness and us is a perspective that can and should be changed. It is as much in error as seeing heart and mind, reason and feeling, body and soul as separate here on Earth. That perspective will change when we accept that the God in human consciousness is us. The currently disjoined concept that we have needs to be brought together by humans physically on this earth, as we need to individually bring ourselves together. Perhaps also while we're physically here on this earth."

"We as individuals need to bring the dreamer and the dream, the subconscious and the conscious together in our individual lives. The same way we need to bring our awareness of our sensorial capabilities into conscious realization, not leave them as a vague feeling or an urge," says Laurel.

"We need to bring our individual overview together with our individual self as humans need to bring our human overview we're calling the God in human consciousness together with humanity," says Anoo.

"You're saying the connections we've been talking about happen within individual consciousness. An individual consciousness that includes our soul. We should use those connections to bring our awareness of who we are, as individuals, into our physical consciousness," says Cassie.

"We should use those connections to bring any disjoined parts of ourselves together within our physical consciousness," says Jed.

"You're saying those connections happen beyond time and distance in our individual human consciousness. Our individual human consciousness includes consciousness after death," says Eli. "Human souls presumably existing in a place beyond time and distance. When we have an experience that goes beyond time and distance we're connecting with our souls."

"Our human souls are connected to us physically on this planet. That is why we are able to grow our own souls with the right quality of thought and feeling," says Tohlee. "I say well done, Anoo—let's regroup for a bit."

"Thank you and just one more quick comment. I'd like to say that this topic makes sense to us because of the base, the value systems, the perspective that we as individuals have. A perspective that we have intentionally created in ourselves with our own awareness. My mother and father have fostered that perspective in me. I thank you both and also Mateen for helping me be who I am now," says Anoo.

"I'd like to thank my grandfather, Grandfather," says Laurel with a smile.

"Thank you, Cassie. You've added purpose and value to my life to a degree I didn't know I could have before knowing you," says Jed.

"And right back at you, my loving man," says Cassie.

"I'd like to thank you, Tohlee, for all you've given me. And you, Anoo, for showing how independent and strong a growing person can become," says Eli.

"Tohlee would say the same to you, Eli and Anoo, if she wasn't quietly crying," says Laurel.

The next day's sunny morning has brought the hummingbirds and butterflies to Tohlee's garden. They make for excellent company as everyone enjoys a big breakfast in preparation for the coming day's work. Eli and Anoo have decided it's a good day to harvest the hay meadow for the second time this season. It's a little more than an acre and will be a good winter supply of hay for the two horses. They'll be able to be out in their pasture until early winter and then will need the stored hay for a few months. The harvest will be done by hand since the meadow isn't that large. The cutters will take turns with the large scythes necessary for the harvest. Anoo and Eli start cutting while everyone else works on veggies. An hour or so of cutting and it's time for Jed and Laurel to take a turn. With some pointers from Anoo it doesn't take long for Laurel to learn how to use the scythe efficiently. As she's cutting Anoo rakes some paths through the cut hay. The paths allow the workers to move about the meadow without stepping on the fresh-cut hay. They also expose the mice that have been living under a couple feet of standing greens. As the scent of fresh-cut hay fills the air a marsh hawk starts to circle the field. It flies low, looking for mice disturbed by the cutting. Anoo is surprised to see the bird leave without making a kill. He looks around and sees why. A red-tail is flying in. It lands on a fence post and watches the activity intently. After Laurel's turn cutting they break for water. Walking down a path Laurel and Anoo see a mouse come up onto the cut hay a few feet in front of them. The red-tail sees it too and hops excitedly on the fence post but doesn't fly. When the mouse is thirty feet from the couple the hawk decides it's safe enough. The bird jumps off the post and is moving fast with only a couple flaps of its wings and the momentum from the little drop off the post. Laurel and Anoo get a great view of the underside of the hawk's extended wings as it nears the mouse. The mouse makes a last quick, defensive zigzag, but it isn't enough. The hawk's talons make a quick reflexive grab and the mouse is taken into the air with a final squeak. They watch as the hawk flies to a cottonwood. When they come back from their water break the hawk is back on its fence post watching for more easy meals.

When the cutting is finished everyone takes a well-deserved break. Over the next couple of days, the hay will be raked so it dries evenly and will then be moved to the barn loft. From there it will be forked down to the horses as needed. After the break the day's veggie work is completed and then there's time for swimming and sweating. When everyone is sweated clean and relaxed they go to the flower garden to watch the sphinx moths trade places with the butterflies and hummingbirds. The meditative activity is all anyone wants to do for a while. In time, they move to the porch to watch the last of the sunset and talk.

"I think we've covered a lot of ground and need a recap of where we are now," suggests Jed.

"We started working on connections," says Cassie.

"There were five examples. Empathy and telepathy were two," says Laurel.

"We decided those are too closely related to look at each separately. To some people it may seem the pathway is different because they're more experienced with one or the other. We're deciding it's the same pathway. They both have their use. It's possible the clearer the thinking the greater a person's likelihood to use telepathy. What matters most is they both go beyond time and distance," says Tohlee.

"There's knowing when a person is looking at you even when that person hasn't been seen or heard," says Eli.

"I think that one is very similar to projecting one's sensorial awareness away from the body. I think the same method of projection is used but with sensorial awareness not fully engaged. The reaching out I think is the same," says Anoo.

"That would be for the looker, not the person sensing they're being watched. For the person being watched, I think the realization they are being watched is through a telepathic type of awareness," says Laurel.

"In each case the process covers distance in a way that seems to take no time," says Eli.

"I want to leave open the possibility that the process goes beyond time. The evidence is my knowing what I will find hours later in the day," says Anoo.

"I think the prescience needed for that to occur shows the process goes beyond time because you're saying the process will result with a particular find in the future. We don't want to preclude the possibility just to conveniently reach a conclusion," says Laurel.

"There's looking someone in the eye from a distance and having the impression that person's eyes are right in front of you. That's distance covered but not time, I guess," says Cassie.

"Are those all the examples?" asks Tohlee.

"There's the dream connection. What is connecting to what when we wake in a dream that we've been having? What connects us to our bodies when we are dreaming and are away from our body?"

"When we're in a realized dream away from the body there is a direct connection. A connection between our body and our awareness that is away from the body. For the connection between dreamer and dream, the connection is there and then we become aware the connection is being used," says Tohlee.

"Let's first recognize the similarity between intentionally sending our awareness away from the body, shown with Anoo's rock specimen examples, and realizing our awareness is away from our body in a dream state," says Eli.

"In each case we become aware of something we're already doing," says Anoo.

"They may be similar but different. Either way there is a distance factor. Prescience in dreams or visions has a long history, so reaching beyond time is also a factor," says Jed.

"We also have the connection of our physical selves with an overview of our life on Earth. Then there's the connection of our physical selves with an overview of us from a perspective beyond death," says Cassie.

"That may be the same connection," Jed suggests. "It depends on where the source is and we're saying we need to actively explore where that connection is coming from."

"We need to actively explore all these connections that go beyond time and distance. We're trying not to reach conclusions without supporting evidence," agrees Cassie.

"There's the connection with what Anoo termed the God in human consciousness. Humans need to realize that phenomenon is us. Not an entity acting on us, not an entity separate from us. In the long run that's for all of humanity to accomplish. In the meantime, there is a connection there and it also is an overview. We can't rejoin the God in human consciousness with human consciousness through our own individual effort. We, as individuals, need to create conscious awareness of what we are connected to that goes beyond time and distance. That will create an awareness of who we already are and what we are already connected to. I think we're deciding that directness and clarity through intent in our daily lives will help increase that conscious awareness of the parts of us that can reach beyond time and distance. I think we're deciding that focusing on connections that reach beyond time and distance is an area of the human condition that holds enormous potential. I think we're deciding we've created a base through directness and clarity that we can build on as we continue to explore the incredible mystery of our individual potential. I hope I haven't spoken out of turn," says Eli.

"I don't think so," says Tohlee.

"I think we're all in agreement," says Cassie. "As Anoo said yesterday, to increase our awareness of the parts of ourselves that can reach beyond time and distance we need to reinforce the times we do perceive beyond time and distance. We've all had those experiences. When we have those experiences, we need to consciously realize it's happening. After the experience we need to go back over what happened mentally and physically where appropriate. We're very connected. We act with depth that we're not consciously aware of. We have memories of our actions that can be brought into our consciousness."

"We have memories that extend beyond the conscious awareness we're acting from at the time of these events. We are more than we think we are. We may have spirit guides helping us, we do have our inquisitive natures, and we have our desire to be clear and direct," says Anoo.

"Spirit guides, angels, and the ancestors all being different societal takes on the same phenomenon. Basically, help from beyond the physical. Our various overviews are also available to help us. We're more than we commonly realize we are. We have more interaction that extends beyond time and distance than we commonly realize. An overall philosophy would be that increasing individual awareness of self creates individual evolutionary momentum. With enough individual momentum societal momentum can be achieved," Eli concludes.

"Very well said, my loving man," says Tohlee.

"And now we should go off and explore," says Laurel.

"And report back with our successes and failures as we try to become more aware of what we already are," says Anoo.

"With the understanding that when one is nonviolent and holds the value systems of 'do unto others' and that anger doesn't validate perspective there is a limit to the error that can be made," says Eli.

"And so, a limit to the debt that can be incurred from the over-view of our soul. The soul that we are here to grow," says Cassie.

"Let's have a drink," suggests Jed.

"We do have a lot of work to do tomorrow," reminds Tohlee.

"That's why we're going to drink and dance and have naked plea-sures tonight," says Cassie with an impudent younger sister tone.

"Eli, Cassie is being sassy. Please dirty dance with me so I can ignore her," requests Tohlee.

"Don't we need music and a drink first?" asks Eli.

"If you don't get up it's going to be a lap dance," cautions Tohlee.

"I'm good either way," says Eli conclusively. "No, I definitely want both," he adds just as conclusively.

After some partying to change the mood and going to the loft to share naked pleasures Anoo falls asleep. Laurel relaxes and thinks back on her day. She's worked hard and enjoyed the company of the friends who are her new family. She's spent the day with her loving man. After singing and dancing she created in him a lust she used to satisfy herself. It's time for restful sleep. A rest that begins deep and then is interrupted by awareness. She knows where she is. She's comfortable here. She knows she's resting. Sitting up she finds her arm is on Anoo's. His body doesn't stir but she feels his movement. She thinks his name and sees his face in her mind where she dreams. He sits up. She looks at him until she knows he's aware of her and where they are. She takes his hand and thinks herself standing. Anoo follows. She thinks of the view out the loft window looking down toward the river. They're up on the roof of the barn, looking down. Looking down from up high like birds that can't fall. Anoo is gone. He was just here. She knows he's back in bed. She moves her physical hand and she is back in bed too. She touches his arm and leans over and kisses his cheek. Anoo realizes he's back in bed. He remembers where he was and how Laurel took him to the roof. He remembers he had a moment of doubt, a quick feeling of fear, and he found himself back in bed not quite asleep. He wonders if Laurel is disappointed in him and feels her touch and then her kiss on his cheek. After setting himself up with a reminder to remember in the morning he goes to sleep.

At first light Anoo wakes to find Laurel looking at him.

"I remember you took me up onto the roof. I guess I wasn't ready to stay up there with you."

"It wasn't me you didn't want to be with. You reacted to an unfamiliar perspective."

"I think I should have been willing to stay there because you were there."

"Even with me right there it is a very individual experience. You went back to where you are most familiar perceiving from. You didn't go away from me."

"When I send myself out on a string and perceive away from my body I'm focused on something like a rock specimen or an animal. Last night there was just me perceiving out into the world, not toward something in particular. The experience was greater in scope than I'm used to. I think I can do better next time. Were you disappointed?"

"I'm not sure what I would have done next if you had stayed with me. I think that your realizing you were there and able to remember this morning is a step that we can build on. I also think that the next time you should focus on me as a warm and comforting friend instead of realizing the unexplored enormity around you. We can see what happens next time."

"You are my warm and comforting friend."

"I guess I need to reinforce that truth. How can I wrap myself around you with warmth and good feelings?"

After some good-natured ribbing on what made Anoo and Laurel late for breakfast everyone settles in to another workday. Progress is certainly being made. Empty rows are scattered throughout the garden, root cellar shelves are filling, drying racks are full under the afternoon sun. With work winding down for the day Anoo and Laurel go down to the river to start the fire for the sweat lodge. When Anoo stops to look at the river from behind his favorite willow Laurel sees that something has caught his attention. She peeks around his shoulder to see.

"It's an otter! I've never seen an otter before," Laurel says excitedly.

Anoo smiles as the otter turns and looks at the willow, wondering why it made a noise.

"Oh! I didn't mean to do that. Will he leave?"

"I don't think so," whispers Anoo. "They feel safe out in the water."

"Do you see them often?"

"Sometimes. Usually every year there's some hanging around for a while. I think they move on after they catch most of the fish in one area."

"He's got something, Anoo!"

They watch as the otter goes to the far shore with what looks like a foot-long sucker.

"I have an idea, Laurel. He's going to stay and eat for a while. Why don't you try to tell the others, telepathically, to come down and watch?"

"Okay, who should I try to contact?"

"You decide, whoever you think you can make contact with."

"I guess that would be Tohlee. Give me a second."

"What do you think?"

"I don't think it worked. I didn't feel a connection."

"Try again. Think about how you feel about her friendship. See her face with your imagination, in a visual daydream."

"I think that was better. But maybe all I did was cause her to wonder if she should have noticed something."

"Do the same thing again, but this time with the burst of excitement you felt when you first saw the otter."

"I think that worked! I reached out toward her with the excitement I felt and I said 'come and see the otter' from within my mind. I think she's on her way."

"What is it, Tohlee?" asks Cassie as she sees Tohlee stop and stare toward the river.

"I think we should go down to the river. Laurel wants us to see something or see if we can help her."

"Laurel wants us to help her?"

"I think so. I'll tell Eli she wants us."

"I'll tell Jed she needs help."

Eli stops what he's doing and sees Jed jogging toward him.

"Eli, does Laurel need help?"

"I think she wants us down at the river. There go the girls."

As all four near the river they can see Anoo and Laurel looking out into the river and they don't look like they need help. When they get closer Anoo turns and motions to be quiet. Walking slowly up to the willow everyone takes turns peeking around it to watch the otter eat. When the otter is finished and starts to clean his face with his paws everyone moves away from the river.

"Did you hear me, Tohlee?" asks Laurel.

"I did, and I told Cassie verbally, who told Jed telepathically. I told Eli telepathically."

"I heard you say we should go to the river," says Eli.

"I thought there was a problem Laurel needed help with," says Jed.

"I was trying to say to come and see the otter," says Laurel. "I didn't mean to worry anyone."

"I think I might have played a part in that," says Anoo. "Tohlee, did you reach out to me because Laurel tried to contact you?"

"I think I did now that you mention it. I was trying to learn what was happening."

"And I think, looking back on it, I said to you that Laurel needed help. I meant she needed help with experiencing a telepathic connection."

"The help part is what I passed on to Jed. I didn't get anything about an otter," says Cassie.

"And that's why Jed came up to me with more concern than I had," realizes Eli.

"What an interesting interaction," says Tohlee. "It really was like a normal conversation with all the possibilities of miscommunication when everyone isn't being clear."

"There is no ethical value system inherent in telepathy. It's the individual's ethical system that is in play. There can be miscommunication, deception, lies, or intentional misleading just like talking out loud. It depends on the individual characters of the people involved," says Eli.

"Truth is in the eye of the beholder. Truth is not in hierarchical structures or organized religions or societal leanings. In the same way accuracy in telepathic communication is not found in the method of communication itself. It is in what is communicated by the individuals involved. Clarity and being direct are as important for telepathic communication as verbal communication. Deceit, manipulation, and lies can all be communicated by telepathy if that is what is desired by the individuals involved," says Anoo in summary.

"That was well said, Anoo. Will you get the fire going? I want a sweat and Mr. Otter is done eating," says Cassie.

After everyone has a sweat and dinner is cooking, the conversation about the afternoon communication continues.

"There may not be an ethical system inherent in telepathy but I did have to reach a level of clarity and energy to reach Tohlee. A level that isn't necessary with most verbal communication," notes Laurel.

"I think the effort decreases with familiarity of contact," says Eli. "It's after reaching familiarity of contact that the deceit possible in communication can happen, even with telepathy."

"That deceit isn't a concern for us. It's if our little circle of communication expanded out to the wrong person that it would be a problem," says Tohlee.

"There's always people with wrong intentions out there. I think that, most of the time, those people should just be avoided. Trying to help them to be better people can be a full-time job that is often resented," says Jed.

"Who are those people?" asks Laurel.

"We know how to characterize many of them," says Cassie. "People who are too hypocritical to live by the Golden Rule."

"People who think anger validates perspective," adds Anoo.

"Anyone who hasn't grown beyond their feelings and so still thinks their feelings are The Truth. As compared to seeing feelings as a current truth based on one's own perspective, knowledge, experiences, baggage, and value systems," continues Tohlee.

"Those same people judge with their feelings first and learn and communicate second," says Jed.

"People who don't live Constitutional Freedoms on an individual level are too intolerant to develop a broad-based perspective," says Laurel.

"The overall view is that people who find truth in organizations or hierarchies instead of in themselves end up lacking in individual perspective. It's the same for the hierarchy of politics. People who can't prove the validity of their own political perspective and so criticize another political party or politician are too weak in their political perspective to be efficient leaders even if they do come into political power," says Tohlee.

"There's the head-butting, pissing contest types. Those people are acting from their feelings, not proof of perspective. They hide their insecurity and lack of perspective behind aggression," says Eli. "I think I know a way to see early on in a conversation if the interaction with that person will be good or not."

"That could certainly be beneficial. What are you thinking?" asks Tohlee.

"Be clear and direct, straight and honest, however you want to term it."

"As we all try to do, and then?"

"First, I'm not talking about a tense conversation. I mean any common interaction."

"Okay, I'm following," says Tohlee.

"If the person recognizes you're dealing straight, being honest, and builds on that, great."

"And if not?"

"If they feel the need to reinterpret your direct and clear comment there's going to be misunderstanding and discomfort," Eli replies.

"In the same conceptual way as accepting one value system instead of another can result, over time, with a person becoming a different individual. Reinterpretation will result in a different conversation. A conversation much more likely to include misunderstandings."

"That's right," agrees Eli. "If the person recognizes the straight, honest communication then all is well. If they don't, if they think they're in a conversation that they need to interpret—interpret with their feelings instead of listening to the specific words chosen by the person trying to deal straight—there will be misunderstandings."

"You're talking about when a person doesn't listen to the specific words in a conversation but instead gets a general impression of what's being said. If everyone is being as vague as everyone else, then fine. If someone is being specific and is interpreted vaguely there will be misunderstandings," says Tohlee.

"I am," Eli agrees. "I'm also saying that in vagueness there is the opportunity for intentional skewing, deceit, manipulation."

"Negative forms of communication," Anoo interjects.

"I think we've covered characterizations of people who drain the energy away from those who are trying to stand on their own perspective. Let's eat and drink and dance," suggests Tohlee.

"First, I'd like to thank Anoo and Laurel for giving us, as a group, the opportunity to experience how we can be our own validation of our experiences," says Eli.

"We achieved that by comparing notes after the fact," says Jed.

"And by remembering things we weren't quite aware of even though we were acting on them," adds Cassie.

"Okay, now it's time to eat, drink, and dance," reminds Tohlee.

"Tomorrow Jed and I should go back to town. We'd rather stay because of good company, good work, exploring potential, food, drink, and play," says Cassie.

"Unfortunately, our life in town calls. Thank you all for a great experience," says Jed.

"And thank you, Anoo, for bringing Laurel into all our lives," says Cassie.

"I think it's time for some 'including moderation' in the everything in moderation saying," says Eli.

After an evening of revelry everyone sleeps in. Still, the morning sun has barely risen above the horizon when the farmers start to stir. While Eli makes one of his big breakfasts everyone else goes out to Tohlee's flower garden to watch the butterflies and hummingbirds begin their morning. They sit and relax in the morning sun and Tohlee's oldest cat walks up to her for some behind-the-ears scratching and then moves to Anoo and climbs up in his lap.

"Oh, oh," say Tohlee and Cassie in unison.

"What's oh, oh?" say Laurel and Jed in unison and they both laugh.

"Tohlee has always been that cat's favorite and he just chose to go to Anoo," says Cassie.

"Why is that a concern?" asks Laurel.

"Animals who know they aren't long for this earth seem to seek out Anoo. It may be months, but a statement was made," says Tohlee with remorse.

"Why do animals seek you out when they sense their time here is drawing near?" asks Laurel.

"I don't know," says Anoo.

"It's a pattern we've seen before," says Cassie.

"Maybe it has to do with the number of animal spirits I've felt as I've taken their life for food," suggests Anoo.

"But the animals choose you over Eli," notes Tohlee. "And he knows those spirits too."

"That's right. I don't know what the attraction is."

"Tell us more about animal spirits, Anoo," Jed requests.

"I can feel their spirits when they pass and then I see, as though through their eyes, moments of their exuberance," Anoo explains. "A deer running with abandon, the feel of cool water running down a parched throat."

"So it could be moments of intense feeling from life memories," suggests Jed.

"It could be. There is a connection there. I'm not sure how far it reaches. I choose to see it as a connection with the animal's life after death just like I see people having the ability to maintain individual perspective after death."

"There's no reason to rush to a negative conclusion. Why couldn't animals have an afterlife? People are animals and they do," says Laurel.

"The only reason would be human superiority or uniqueness. So, no apparent valid reason," says Cassie.

"Is this another connection we need to explore, Anoo?" asks Jed.

"I think it's basically a telepathic connection. To explore it would give breadth to telepathy but I don't think it's a separate connection."

"I see," says Jed. "Tohlee, I didn't mean to make light of your love for and connection with your cat or to make light of his life by being intellectual about this."

"Thank you for that, Jed. It's okay; it's really more of a wake-up call than a warning of a near future event."

"It means it's time for some special food treats and extra ear scratches," says Cassie.

"Time for more purring lap time," says Laurel.

"Let's change the subject by getting some of Eli's breakfast," suggests Tohlee.

After a big breakfast and warm good-byes Jed and Cassie go back to town. A lot of work has been accomplished but vegetables are ripening daily. It takes most of the rest of the day to take care of the produce ready for harvest. Afterward Anoo and Laurel go down to the river.

"I want to experiment some more before we swim and sweat, Anoo."

"What do you want to do?"

"Let's look at each other from a distance and bring our awareness together," suggests Laurel.

"Okay, I guess here is fine. The first time we were a couple hundred yards apart. We can probably be closer. I'll go over to that cottonwood and you can be by this one."

After getting set Anoo and Laurel look into each other's eyes from about fifty yards apart. They're close enough to see each other but too far apart to hear without calling loudly. They think warm and loving thoughts about each other but the closest they feel occurs when they close their eyes and imagine the other. They want to feel the other's presence through their eyes as though they're standing right in front of each other. After trying for a while Anoo walks up to Laurel.

"That didn't really work. What do you think we did wrong?" he asks.

"Let's increase clarity and directness with motivation."

"How should we do that?"

"Let's think about how we were looking in each other's eyes last

206

night when we were joined." Laurel looks in Anoo's eyes and then pushes him away as he reaches for her. "From your tree, Anoo."

After Anoo walks back to his tree they try again. They look into each other's eyes from a distance again and think about the night before. The partying had finished; they went to their loft and indulged in naked pleasures. They were too tired for energetic coupling. It had been a slow pleasuring while looking into each other's eyes. Now they look at each other and remember the night before. They feel the closeness they had last night. They still don't feel like they are standing in front of each other. Anoo walks back to Laurel.

"That was better but not the full experience I wanted," he says.

"Let's try again. This time let's start with what we just did. After a couple minutes let's increase our motivation by thinking about what we want to do now, not what we did last night," suggests Laurel.

Back at his tree Anoo tries again. He looks at Laurel and focuses on her eyes. He remembers their closeness the night before and then thinks of the warmth he feels when he's inside of his Laurel. He remembers the warmth in his heart, the depth in her eyes. He closes his eyes and they kiss. He pulls her hips toward him and feels that he is aroused as she pushes against him. When he opens his eyes all he sees are Laurel's eyes looking into his own. His heart reaches out and finds hers. He wants to feel her arms reach around him pulling their bodies together. A magpie squawks and Laurel is over by her tree. He walks up to her.

"I'm glad you're as ready as I am, Anoo."

Chapter Eleven

THE NEXT FEW days run together with a nice balance of work and play. Conversations are about the work. Most evenings after dinner the couples enjoy their own company. For entertainment there's sunsets and clouds, flowing water, butterflies and moths, birds, life to watch and live. One evening they all go to the nearest upstream neighbors on their side of the road for dinner. Laurel enjoys meeting and talking to everyone in the family and they enjoy meeting their good friend Anoo's new love.

The most noteworthy exploring for Laurel and Anoo happens when they are looking in each other's eyes from what has become their two favorite cottonwood trees. They find themselves together telepathically but don't talk. They feel themselves looking in each other's eyes as though they are standing right in front of each other. They feel aroused and want consummation and then they are moving. It is as though they are skimming over the earth. They are still looking in each other's eyes but there is green moving in their peripheral vision. They are together, joined, and pleasuring each other with abandon.

"That was extra good even compared to the extra good of last time. How did that happen?" asks Laurel.

"The circumstance. What did we do, Laurel? Did we pull ourselves together with our connection?"

"It didn't feel like we walked towards each other. I felt like I do when I'm out of my body and instead of flying I push off the ground and am almost weightless. I move forward and then when I slowly drop down near the ground I push off again. When I do that I can keep my view of what is going on around me. When I'm flying I usually go too fast to keep my awareness. I end up feeling like I'm moving but I don't know where I'm going until I get there."

"I felt like I was moving. I saw plants as blurry greenery going by me. Then, I was physically with you. I've walked from one tree to the other often enough the last few days that I don't think checking our tracks will help to understand what we did."

"We each did something. That's important to remember," says Laurel.

"If all we did was walk towards each other while telepathically joined and our eyes locked together, why wouldn't we have been aware of our own movements?"

"We weren't aware of our own movements because we did something out of the ordinary for us. I think our desire to couple was motivation for us to move together in the same way I used my excitement at seeing the otter to reach out to Tohlee telepathically the other day."

"So exceptional thoughts and feelings cause us to grow when we're here in the physical and we are growing our souls also."

"Yes, because we are ourselves and our souls at the same time, connected and interacting."

"Well said, my lovely Laurel, well said."

A few days later, the day Laurel has been anticipating dawns. Her grandfather had let her know yesterday evening that today he and Mateen would come to the farm. His contact had been clear and strong. A contact meant to communicate a particular message, not to intrude. Grandfather stayed at the cabin for a few days after Laurel left. Then he went back to summer camp, where Briana and Teresa made sure he was as well cared for as if Laurel were there. Now he's back at the cabin and ready to go to the farm. When Grandfather was at summer camp Mateen visited so everyone could meet him. When

Grandfather returned to the cabin from summer camp Briana and Teresa and a guy from camp walked with him to the cabin and visited for the day so that they knew the way.

At the cabin the first patches of frost have appeared down by Mateen's little stream. The serviceberries are showing their rusty fall leaf color before their early drop, and the chokecherry leaves are turning yellow. It will be a nice day for a walk to the farm. The two older gentlemen are up early as older men often are and on the trail by sunrise. It will be a long walk but there's no need for heavy packs. There will be dinner and friends at the end of the trail.

It's an average mid-September day on the farm. Some plants could use rain, but dry weather is best for harvesting. The day is no different than the last few, but Laurel's sense of time is different due to the anticipation of seeing her grandfather. She's fidgety and even walks to where she can look down the lane to the road a few times. Thankfully, in the early afternoon Anoo suggests a swim and sweat to clean up and then a walk to town. When they get to town they stop in at the library to say hello to Cassie. They go to the tavern and sit outside where they can watch the trail running down from the lake and along the river. As they wait, Anoo introduces Laurel to the people at the tavern. They talk about the possibility of meeting the singles at summer camp and who should go. The conversation about who's currently adventurously available is perfect for passing time at the tavern.

After a couple of hours of enjoyable conversation Anoo sees Mateen and Grandfather drop down the face of the dam and start to walk along the river. Laurel runs to her grandfather to give him a welcoming hug. Mateen hasn't been through town for several months, so everyone at the tavern is glad to say hello. There's introductions for Grandfather and offers of drinks. Mateen and Grandfather are both a little dry and so stay for a drink. Anoo knows Eli and Tohlee are waiting at the farm and insists they get going after that. Two hours later and they're at the farm and settling in on the porch as the sun is starting to set. There's lots to talk about. Laurel wants to know everything that's been happening at camp, Mateen with the harvest, and Anoo can share the current goings-on in town. They talk through dinner as the sun sets and then it's bedtime for the weary walkers.

The next day the two walkers are a little too stiff for a full day of harvesting. They enjoy a leisurely breakfast as everyone else works on the day's harvest. After his breakfast Laurel and Anoo show Grandfather around the farm. He's very impressed with the setup and the amount of produce already stored and still in the fields. He's not the winter camp's gardening expert as he spends summers at summer camp. He is familiar with some of the types of veggies grown here while others are new to him. Anoo is impressed with his questions about soil needs, companion planting, and storage ability. From Grandfather's questions Anoo starts to get an idea of how he can help the winter camp's gardens and what seeds to bring with him. Later in the day it's time for a nature walk along the river. Grandfather wonders aloud about how close the fields are to the wildlife that uses the river corridor as a travel route. Anoo explains how important the dogs are for wildlife patrols. How most of the local wild animals have learned where they can go and be left alone and where they'll attract the dogs' attention. After everything that is ready to be harvested for the day is out of the fields and in the process of being stored Anoo sets Grandfather and Mateen up with a sweat. Tomorrow will be a better day for a full day's work. Now it's time for everyone to relax in the flower gardens and enjoy each other's company.

"What have you guys been talking about after we left?" asks Laurel. "You've had a lot of time to visit."

"A lot of different things," replies Mateen.

"On the walk here I was thinking about how closely animal behaviors can reflect human behavior," says Grandfather.

"That sounds interesting. What did you come up with?" asks Anoo.

"What examples of tool use by animals have you seen?" asks

Grandfather and continues with his own example. "I've seen seagulls along the big river by our town drop mussel shells from a height onto rocks and if they don't break right away they go get them and take them back up to drop again until the shell breaks and they can eat."

"So that would be kind of a hammer and anvil used to break the shell. The velocity from falling is the effect of the hammer, and the rocks the mussel falls on are the anvil," says Anoo and gives an example himself. "I've seen both hairy and downy woodpeckers wedge sunflower seeds into bark furls on locust trees and then break them open for the nut inside."

"That would be using the furls as a vise. Why not just hold them in their feet like chickadees do?" asks Laurel.

"I think the structure of their bodies. I don't think they can get their beak on the seeds the way chickadees can," explains Anoo.

"I've seen grasshoppers impaled on plum thorns by shrikes. I think they do that for food storage. I don't think it's to kill the grasshopper," contributes Laurel and after considering, "I guess I haven't seen them actually do the impaling. I'm not sure if the grasshoppers are already dead or not."

"Then how do you know it was shrikes that did it?" asks Anoo.

"Because Grandfather said so," says Laurel with tongue sticking out conviction.

"I have actually seen them do it. I think the shrikes give the grasshoppers a hard bite when they catch them. They're probably at least incapacitated," says Grandfather.

"Hopefully, for the grasshopper, the thorn finishes them off," says Laurel.

"The shrike is at least using the thorn as a drying rack of sorts, even if it's not being used as a weapon," says Mateen.

"Does a pika count as a tool user?" wonders Anoo. "They cut hay, dry it in the sun, move it under cover when it rains and then back out to dry after the shower passes. They store the dry hay for the winter."

"That's certainly a more active and involved use of the sun than a lizard warming itself. Are we interested in a tool that is held or complex behavior that benefits survival?" asks Tohlee.

"I'm interested in examples of either," says Grandfather.

"I've seen a badger's hibernation burrow have a front door made of an antelope skull a couple times," says Anoo.

"They know they're going in for the winter and close themselves in with the skull?" asks Laurel.

"Yes, and there's been no meat left on the skull so it's not for a later meal."

"It wouldn't be wise for them to use a skull that still smells as it could bring predators to their winter sleep home," says Eli.

"That's a good point. I've also seen foxes and coyotes hunt to-gether," says Anoo.

"Hunt together meaning side by side?" asks Laurel.

"This is more complex. I've seen one of a pair circle ahead to the end of a draw and then the second, which was waiting for the first to get in position, move up the draw trying to push prey to the first that is waiting."

"That is certainly complex," Laurel comments.

"I've also seen a rufous-sided towhee watch the far side of a ser-viceberry bush as a green-tailed towhee goes into the bush on the ground. I don't think that's mutually beneficial though," says Anoo.

"It sounds more opportunistic for the rufous, but it is interesting because two species are involved. As compared to the mutually hunt-ing foxes and coyotes that were probably paired up and benefitting each other as parents or future parents," says Laurel.

"I've always thought they were paired up when I've seen it," says Anoo. "I've also seen mule deer bucks raise their heads up into juni-per tree branches to hide them from me, the hunter."

"Are you sure it was intentional?"

"The hillside was rocky with small shrubs and only a couple juni-per trees. The buck changed direction to get over to one of the trees when it could have chosen to run. If you had seen the buck move his head up and his antlers disappear into the branches you'd have prob-ably thought it deliberate also."

"For the two species interacting category I've seen magpies feeding on ticks from the ears of deer. I've also seen blackbirds hitch a ride on the backs of wild horses and fly off to get a bug disturbed by the hooves of the horses and then fly back to ride the horse some more," says Grandfather.

"What about beaver that build a wooden structure to put the waterproofing of mud on when they build ponds?" asks Mateen.

"That's certainly complex; it may not be tool use but they are building a multipart structure," says Anoo.

"How about when a pair of robins chase another pair of robins out of their territory?" asks Grandfather and then answers his own question. "Maybe that's not complex behavior. I'm not sure there is a two-bird strategy, just two birds acting in concert."

"Not a strategy or ploy like two foxes hunting. Those territorial fights are so quick it's hard to tell who's doing what and why," says Eli.

"From an animal behavior that reflects human behavior standpoint I heard tool use and how parents work together to provide for their children," says Tohlee.

"Also, food storage for the winter and defending their home territory from competitors," says Laurel.

"Teaching their young to fend for themselves and how to communicate with others," adds Anoo.

"They do things for enjoyment like otters playing." Tohlee smiles.

"I'm thinking that, in their own way, animals do a lot of the things people do. Just like different people do the same things others do but in their own way," says Eli.

"You're talking about how different people have their own way of making a living, keeping a house, and raising children," says Tohlee.

"Maybe the difference is that it takes many different species of animals to equal the variety of methods people use to survive?" Anoo suggests.

"That might apply for most animals. From what I have read in the library, that wouldn't be true for chimpanzees. They do things like use tools, teach and provide for their children, and organize for war to defend their territory," says Eli.

"I think people have to intend to apply themselves to function above the level of animals. That level of functioning is not a gift that causes the behavior to be innate," says Grandfather.

"Especially if you look at that level of behavior from the standpoint of how much effort it can take for humans to keep from projecting negatives like hate, anger, and bigotry on to others," says Tohlee.

"Not to mention how hard it is for people to keep war or any physical violence out of their behavior," adds Eli.

"Or how common it's been throughout human history for humanity to spend its future on war over and over and over again," says Mateen and then changes the subject. "What have you guys been talking about? I understand Cassie and Jed were here for a while."

"We talked a lot about connections," says Laurel.

"What sort of connections?" asks Grandfather.

"Connections that go beyond time and/or distance," says Anoo.

"What are some examples?"

"Telepathic or empathic connections. What actually connects with what."

"What connects when two people look each other in the eye from a distance and it's as though they're standing right next to each other," says Laurel.

"When a person feels like they're being watched and then they turn around and find they actually are. What is it that reaches out and connects from one to the other?" asks Eli.

"That's sure more involved than what I was thinking about," Grandfather comments with a little chagrin.

"I think how animal behaviors can be similar to people behavior is very interesting," says Eli.

"Conversations don't need to be deep and complex to be enjoyed. There are always learning opportunities in any conversation," says Tohlee. "I think the detailed understanding that is necessary to teach and to explain to others can go beyond what is necessary for individual learning."

"There is a balance there. Knowing defined by a feeling is self-centered compared to knowing defined by explanation," says Eli.

"Giving the opportunity for others to learn requires a clear understanding in the teacher," says Mateen.

"Or else the supposed teacher will sink down into 'don't think—obey,' showing an inability to actually teach," says Anoo.

"*Don't think—obey* is a sinking-down to authoritarianism, being right by position, not proof," says Laurel.

"I also think a person can get lost in detail and so not fully realize a potential learning," says Tohlee.

"I think that's where the direct part of clear and direct comes in," says Eli. "Unnecessary detail isn't direct and can lead to lengthy explanations that lose context."

"Error can be found in going too far in either direction. There's a balance as Eli pointed out. People can get lost in detail and so not explain themselves well. Others may consider only themselves and so not develop the understanding of their own perspective in a way that allows them to explain it to others. Those people define knowing as a feeling, not the ability to explain to others," says Tohlee.

"A feeling of understanding or a feeling of 'getting it'?" asks Laurel.

"That's what I mean," replies Tohlee.

"I think half the things I had to relearn when I was trying to develop my own independent perspective were things authority figures came up with when they couldn't prove their points but needed to feel like they were in control," says Grandfather.

"That is such an odd process," says Eli. "The authority figure is asked a question and pretends they know something they don't. Usually they create in themselves, based on their position, a feeling of knowing others can perceive. A feeling that is more about commanding than actually knowing. The people the authority figures are talking to pretend that if an authority figure pretends they know something they don't then things are better."

"That is really odd. Why doesn't the authority figure just say they don't know?" asks Tohlee and then answers herself. "Of course it's because they need to be in authority. Some people, even as adults, still need the authoritative airs parents put on for young children."

"Followers and leaders are links in the same chain and so subject to each other's weaknesses," says Eli.

"That process of pretending to know gives value to skepticism," says Anoo.

"Pretending to know something belittles the person you're talking to," says Mateen.

"Relearning is a more involved process than learning. One has to undo before learning. The quicker a parent can get to 'I don't know' with their child the less relearning the child will have to do in the future. The longer a child needs an authoritative air the greater the effort needed in the future to develop an independent perspective," says Grandfather.

"Question authority is probably better explained as make authority prove its points. Make the individual who is in authority prove they deserve to hold the position they have," says Laurel.

"Don't flock with adults who are mollified by authority. You'll become substandard and boring," says Mateen.

"Where did you guys end up on connections?" asks Grandfather.

"We all experience them, we need more experiences for greater understanding, and we need to share our experiences for support," says Eli.

"The mind is where the connections happen; the heart is more of an ethical structure for the mind. Perceiving away from the body on a string that comes from the body may be different," adds Anoo.

"It will be interesting to hear what else you come up with. The way you're characterizing those connections as beyond time and/or distance brings seemingly different topics together in a unique way," says Grandfather.

"I'd like to hear more about your view on Jesus and Christianity, Anoo. You've said to me that you have no problem with the teachings of Jesus but the religion doesn't impress you much," says Tohlee.

"I don't have a problem with most of the teachings of Jesus. I often have a problem with the religion people have built around Jesus and his teachings," replies Anoo.

"Any interpretation by a disciple or any other person is still exactly that, a person's interpretation, and does not have the same value to me as the teachings of Jesus or any of the other great teachers," says Mateen.

"Jesus was Jesus; it's people that built Christianity," says Grandfather.

"When authority figures built the Christian religion, they used too many commands and not enough explanations," says Anoo.

"They tried to fill in gaps where they just should have said they don't know," says Tohlee.

"I like where Jesus said, 'In my father's house there are many mansions, I go to prepare a place for you,'" Anoo comments.

"That doesn't sound like an exclusive path to heaven through Jesus," says Mateen.

"I think proponents of the Christian religion would say the exclusiveness of heaven for Christians came later in Jesus's life and so they think it's more accurate," says Anoo.

"Showing that Jesus became who he did through a process of learning, changing, and growing," says Eli.

"If Jesus sits at the right hand of God the father almighty and judges the quick and the dead, does Jesus judge by his teachings, or those of the Christian religion?" asks Anoo.

"Which Christian religion?" asks Laurel rhetorically.

"If an individual Christian is born again, or imbued with the spirit of Jesus, do they automatically gain the individual character development that would come from applying the teachings of Jesus over decades in one's life?" asks Eli.

"The answer to that is clearly no, going by the actions of so many born again Christians. They commit acts of violence, project anger, act deceitfully, and don't 'do unto others' as commonly as non-Christians," says Tohlee.

"They spend their futures on war just like people of other

religions," says Mateen.

"How about rich people and the eye of the needle?" asks Laurel.

"Still as valid now as ever. Wealth is about having few wants, not many possessions," says Grandfather.

"Wealth is about health, a loving family and friends, and peace, not physical possessions," Tohlee adds.

"The people who have the most to learn from the 'eye of the needle' teaching are the ones most likely to think they're an exception to the teaching," says Mateen.

"How about render unto Caesar what is Caesar's and unto God what is God's?" asks Laurel.

"Still as valid now as ever," says Mateen with a smile and nod to Grandfather.

"As clear a statement of separation of church and state as one can make," adds Eli.

"Why didn't Jesus promote going to church?" asks Laurel.

"His teachings are about actions in life, not buildings or the wealth it takes to build grand buildings which house altars," answers Anoo.

"When did Jesus ask people to worship him?"

"He didn't," says Mateen.

"When did Jesus say to put a person, a pope for example, or a guru or wise man in between an individual and their own process of learning, changing, and growing?"

"He didn't," says Grandfather with a smile and nod to Mateen.

"When did Jesus say to go to an authority figure for forgiveness?" asks Laurel.

"He didn't," Mateen and Grandfather say at the same time and with a laugh.

"If Jesus were here today what would he teach?"

"The same things he taught already. His teachings wouldn't change just because some people don't want his teachings to be current truths," says Tohlee.

"Does being imbued with the spirit of Jesus increase the accuracy of one's political perspective, turn anger into righteousness, or legitimatize violence?" asks Laurel.

"No," says everyone emphatically as they get up to stretch.

"Laurel likes her speed rounds," Anoo comments as he stands.

"Dinner is about ready. Eli, will you help me?" asks Tohlee.

"I'm going to have to charge you a kiss and a hug!"

"We'll have dessert later, my loving man."

After dinner, and before Eli and Tohlee have dessert, Laurel lets Anoo know that Grandfather would like to go down to the river again. Everyone decides to go and soon they're standing by the sweat lodge next to Anoo's swimming hole. Grandfather says that this isn't where he wants to be. After a quick talk with Anoo, Grandfather decides he wants to be a few hundred yards downstream. Anoo knows there is a small bluff there giving a good view over the river to the hills beyond. Grandfather encourages everyone to walk quickly. They've only been at the bluff for a few minutes when Eli points out movement in a clump of hawthorn. Something is shaking the little trees and then eating the thorn apples off the ground. They see enough movement through the trees to know by size that it's a bear, not raccoons. Then it steps out into the open.

"That's a grizzly," says Eli.

"It's a young one," says Anoo, "probably on its own for the first time."

"Do you see them often?" asks Laurel.

"At most one a year," replies Anoo.

"I don't see them any more than that in the hills," adds Mateen.

"We rarely see them at summer camp and never have at winter camp," says Laurel.

"How did you know, Grandfather," asks Tohlee.

Grandfather doesn't answer and when everyone looks at him they know he's concentrating and give him time.

"He wanted contact. He wanted to know where he could go

safely," Grandfather says a little distantly.

Laurel waits a minute and asks, "Are you in telepathic contact with it?"

"He's moving on now and he is young."

"Why is he here?" asks Mateen.

"This past winter was his first hibernation away from his mother. He's been looking for his own territory since spring. I told him to stay on his side of the river and to go south into the hills."

"Told him? In English?" asks Eli.

"Empathy is mostly feelings; telepathy is mostly words in English. With an animal communication is mostly visual. I sent him images from my mind of the river and then the feeling of danger if he crosses it. Then I added the image of dogs barking. I stopped that imagery and then sent him images of aspen groves and tall shrubs full of berries to the south up in the hills. For good measure I added the feeling of a full belly. That part was easy after your delicious meal, Tohlee. Thank you."

"You're very welcome. Thank you, Grandfather, for showing us this possibility of communication with animals. It is quite a gift."

"We all communicate with animals; this was an extreme example of what we are all capable of."

"Empathy uses feelings, telepathy words. What is the term for using imagery to nonverbally communicate?" wonders Anoo aloud. "I think there should be one."

"Maybe there is a term and we just don't know what it is," says Tohlee as everyone turns and slowly walks back to the farm.

Over the next few days, the work gets done along with a good measure of relaxing. Everyone enjoys getting to know Grandfather. Laurel appreciates her time with him even more after her absence from camp. Too soon for her it's time to talk about what happens next. Grandfather tells everyone what he's been thinking during an evening sunset watch on the porch.

"I'm thinking I should get back to summer camp pretty soon," says Grandfather.

"You won't be able to walk very fast dragging me behind you kicking and screaming every step of the way," says Laurel with a loving smile.

"I guess I better get going now then?" Grandfather smiles.

"That didn't work out the way I wanted." Laughs Laurel.

"I'll be staying here another month or so," says Mateen, smiling.

"Laurel and I should walk with Grandfather back to summer camp. We'll go to the cabin the first day and then on to camp the next," says Anoo.

"We can get our timing right with people at camp for an introduction party and our trip to winter camp," says Laurel.

"On the way back to the farm from summer camp you two should stay at the cabin for a few days of togetherness," offers Mateen.

"What a nice idea, Mateen," says Tohlee.

"Thank you, Mateen," say Laurel and Anoo.

"What else did you guys talk about before we got here? Anoo likes to talk about where an individual's truth comes from and how that truth can change as their perspective changes," comments Mateen.

"That is a topic I like. We talked about things where that comes into play," replies Anoo.

"I guess most anything is connected to perspective," says Grandfather. "Get more specific."

"Well, an individual is overly influenced by the first societal truths, including family, political, and religious, they are introduced to at an early age. That influence forms the initial base the individual perceives their perception of truth from," says Anoo.

"So a zygote doesn't have truth yet," comments Laurel with a smile.

"I'm thinking a zygote doesn't contain individual truth. That truth is developed later. The initial base a child adopts from the people around them is supposed to evolve as the child learns and changes and so grows as a person."

222

"That evolution of perspective continues throughout one's life or they developmentally stagnate," says Laurel.

"A child's adoptive values feel like truth. As the child learns and changes and grows, that feeling of truth moves to their new values, their new perspective. The process of growing can cause temporary disorientation, a feeling of loss of truth," says Anoo.

"When the individual learns something novel enough to them to change their perspective they initially feel disoriented. As the new learning is encompassed by the individual and as their experiences validate their new perspective the feeling of truth in their perspective will return. The result of the process is a broader base for the individual to perceive from, to feel their own truths from," says Laurel.

"That process is the same for any truth one feels whether societal, political, or religious," says Anoo.

"The feeling of truth a person has initially goes away, temporarily, during the learning process. It comes back as familiarity with the new perspective grows. A feeling of truth that changes because of something learned is an individual feeling of truth, not a universal truth. Perceptive feelings can change with learning and so can individual truths. In other words, perceptive feelings do not have a godlike level of truth as their source," says Tohlee.

"The source of the feeling of truth in perceptive feelings is the individual. The number of individuals holding the same truths does not add validation to those truths," says Laurel.

"What is perceived as truth is based on individual perspective. That perspective is validated by experience and shown to others by explanation. Perspective is not validated by numbers of people in agreement or the status of who is talking," says Eli.

"Truth is perceived by the individual and is dependent on the individual's base value systems. That base is adopted from the society around the child at first and then that base is created by the individual as they mature through learning, changing, and growing. That is why individuality grows when the value systems used to interpret perceptive feelings are intentionally chosen by the individual," says Anoo.

"Awareness of individually held value systems creates individual perspective," says Laurel.

"Intentionally changing the base an individual perceives truth from is a way to go from reacting to the life around an individual to the individual acting in life," says Tohlee.

"Because truth is determined from a changing base, a base that can change through learning, one can be too quick to pass judgments on others. You may end up learning something about the person that changes your perspective and so invalidates your initial perceptive feeling. If the perceptive feeling was a criticism and voiced you'll owe someone an apology," says Laurel.

"If you've voiced your criticism to others you'll have to go to them and explain your error in perspective. If you don't you'll have promoted a critical perspective of someone in error and let it stand. Even though you don't agree with the critical perspective anymore," says Eli.

"I wouldn't want to be treated that way," says Tohlee.

"Not fixing that error is a statement that the one doing the critiquing deserves the type of critical perspective they directed toward others," says Laurel.

"It's better to learn first and critique later," says Anoo.

"It's better to walk a mile in another's shoes before criticizing them," says Grandfather.

"Critiquing others from an unexamined life is the equivalent of throwing stones from a glass house," says Mateen.

"Today's criticisms can grow into tomorrow's acceptance through learning," says Eli.

"It's best to walk a mile in a new perspective before criticizing from it," says Grandfather with a smile.

"So, perceptive feelings, societal, political, and religious truths are all individual truths because those truths can change with individual learning. Are there universal truths?" Tohlee asks.

"There's the laws of physics," says Eli.

"How about universal religious truths?"

"Maybe in a broad way. A way that encompasses all religions.

The religious truths one is brought up with, or societally surrounded by, can grow through learning. They can grow to the point where the individual becomes a religious independent," says Anoo.

"All those types of truths can grow to the point where the process of creating one's own base to interpret their truth from is the one lasting truth," says Mateen.

"The process that creates the base that truth is perceived from should be an individual action done with awareness and intent. This causes the determiner of one's own truth to have an independent perspective," says Grandfather.

"In the long run that process will result in the awareness that the one constant truth is the individual determination of truth, not the truths themselves which change with learning," says Mateen.

"And some examples of these value system choices that are made by an individual with awareness and so determine the base they interpret truth from?" asks Laurel.

"One would be what we just talked about, don't criticize others before talking to them and learning their circumstance," says Grandfather.

"Don't consider your current base to determine truth from as a truth given by a supreme being. If you do you'll stagnate yourself with self-righteousness," says Mateen.

"Make the choice to learn how to explain yourself so you won't project 'don't think—obey' on the people around you," says Tohlee.

"Don't consider anger to be a validation of perspective," says Eli.

"There are examples that run through what we've enjoyed talking about over the past days and back to when Anoo and I first met," says Laurel.

"I'm wondering what a person is tapping into when their religious feelings strike them as coming from a truth greater than themselves? Is it only bumping up against an established structure?" asks Tohlee.

"It's an established structure based on human consciousness. The structure is not only a religious structure; it also includes the consciousness accumulated by the adherents of the religion, both living and dead. It's the truth of the God in human consciousness split into parts by religion. The God in human consciousness, even split by religion, is a consciousness greater than any one individual," says Anoo.

"That conscious awareness of the God in human consciousness can feel like it is coming from a source greater than the individual because it is. That human consciousness is the accumulation of billions of human lives from a myriad of societies and languages. In this case it would be the subset of human consciousness, living and dead, devoted to a particular religion. The problem, as I see it, is what the individual taps into when they feel religion as a truth beyond themselves. I think what they tap into is usually the most popular and prevalent perspective from the human consciousness that is in the society or individuals around them. It is usually not the arcane perspective of a professor sitting in his study, reaching out to the edge of human knowledge," says Laurel.

"Which is why creating one's individual perspective is better than gaining perspective by reacting to life through one's perceptive feelings. It's why intentionally choosing the value systems one uses to interpret their perceptive feelings is better than letting those values develop in the back of one's mind. What one taps into when they react to life through perceptive feelings that haven't been interpreted by an intentionally developed value system is the average out there in human consciousness. It is not the individual learning or perspective we are all capable of," says Eli.

"The same goes for all societal, political, and religious truths. If a person doesn't intentionally learn their own truths, that individual will be feeling their truth and acting from a perspective that is based on the average out there. Their truth will be based on amount of exposure, not accuracy," says Tohlee.

"Accepting the average perspective out there won't create an individual base to interpret individual truth from. It won't create the opportunity to change from identifying with one's own specific truths to identifying with the process of creating one's own base to interpret truth from," says Mateen.

"That jump in perspective, of finding truth in the process and not in specific truths, that turn on the medicine wheel of life, takes the person to the stability of process. Which increases the speed of learning," says Grandfather.

"We can identify ourselves as, and should strive to identify ourselves as, creators of our own individual base that we identify our own individual truths from. We can learn to see ourselves not as the holders of truths that change through learning but as the process of creating our own truths," says Mateen.

"Throughout that individual learning remember the basics of individual behavior," says Eli.

"Do unto others," says Tohlee.

"Nonviolence," says Anoo.

"Anger doesn't validate perspective," says Laurel.

"The end product of learning is teaching others," says Grandfather.

"Your feelings are your responsibility," says Tohlee.

"You've learned, changed, and grown; others can too," says Laurel.

"Compassion tempers arrogance," says Mateen.

"Constitutional freedoms are granted to all Homo sapien citizens," says Laurel.

"Being American is defined as granting Constitutional freedoms on an individual level," says Eli.

"A tired dog is a good dog," says Anoo, smiling.

"Plant your bulbs with the pointy end up," says Tohlee, laughing.

"Dance like no one is watching," says Laurel as she stands up and twirls.

"I think it's time to eat," says Mateen, feigning exasperation.

The next couple of days pass uneventfully. The only real high point is when a hummingbird lands on Mateen's hand in the butterfly garden and poops on his hand as it flies away. The evening before Grandfather is going to leave everyone settles in on the porch to watch the sunset.

"What would you like to talk about on your last evening with us, Grandfather?"

"Thank you for asking, Tohlee. First, I'd like to say your and Eli's hospitality has been exceptional. I've felt very welcome in your home and I have the highest regard for both of you and Anoo also."

"From all of us, thank you, and we feel the same towards you," replies Tohlee.

"Thank you and I would like to talk about edges," says Grandfather.

"What sort of edges?" asks Tohlee.

"Laurel has told me about your conversations when I wasn't here. Anoo has talked about sensing pieces of petrified wood in a way that seems to go beyond the normal five senses. Although, it may be that he is moving his ability to use his senses away from his body in a way most people aren't familiar with. Either way, when he's doing that he's at the edge of his awareness of his own capability. A part of him is acting in a way that he isn't fully aware of. It takes repeating the occurrence of what he's doing for him to fully realize what he's doing, what he's capable of. That edge of awareness is where individuals can make great strides in understanding who they are. Those edges are everywhere in many different ways in everyone. Close your eyes and intend to hear what is around you and you'll find you can hear more than you realize. You'll find your hearing can produce mental imagery. You can push your sensorial awareness like you can push your physical capabilities. You can push your telepathic ability as you can push your learning about an academic subject. Do research, find out what others say they're capable of. Share your experiences with someone you trust won't ridicule you from the perspective of their own closed mind and you'll both grow," says Grandfather.

"That was well said," Eli commends.

"I'd like to add that one can increase their awareness of themselves by considering 'that's just the way it is' as an invitation to explore," says Mateen.

"I'd like to jump over to feelings," says Laurel. "The feelings that add energy to your soul are more likely to come from feelings you've given others than feelings you've had."

"I'll take thoughts," offers Anoo. "The thoughts that can add energy to your soul are more likely to be thoughts you yourself have."

"That's a difference between thoughts and feelings. Taking into account that difference, thoughts and feelings are meant to work together as part of a whole," says Tohlee.

"I am very grateful for all of you in my life and am very pleased I can share my home with people who bring conversations like we've had into it," says Eli.

The next day Anoo, Laurel, and Grandfather enjoy a nice day-long walk to Mateen's cabin. Along the way they stop at the tavern in town and set a date for a get-acquainted party. It's decided that two men and two women from town will go. After spending the night at the cabin Anoo and Laurel walk with Grandfather to summer camp. Briana and Teresa are enthusiastically willing to stay behind for the party as well as two of the men. Anoo and Laurel decide to spend the night at camp. The next day they go to the cabin for a few days of togetherness. Then it's back to summer camp to say good-bye to Grandfather. When they get there, camp is mostly packed up and the shepherds have already started moving the sheep back toward winter camp. Laurel says good-bye to everyone who's going to winter camp. Laurel and Anoo are going back to the cabin for one more night and then back to the farm. After another month of harvest it's time to go back to Mateen's cabin for the party, which is enjoyed by everyone. The next day at summer camp Anoo finds himself looking back toward the cabin and thinking about the last couple of months. He's met and fallen in love with Laurel. Now he's going east for the winter. The adventure that is his life, the great experiment that is his life, is starting a new chapter.

Lightning Source UK Ltd.
Milton Keynes UK
UKHW020110220219
337759UK00010B/1038/P